Poor Will's
Almanack
for 2018

by

Bill Felker

The sun rises and the sun goes down and hurries to the place where it rises. The wind blows to the south and goes around to the north; round and round goes the wind, And on its circuits the wind returns.

Quoheleth

Copyright 2017 by Bill Felker

Published by the Green Thrush Press
Box 431, Yellow Springs, Ohio

Printed in the United States of America
Charleston, SC – September 2017

ISBN-13: 978-1975863333

ISBN-10: 197586333X

Introductions for Using
Poor Will's Almanack for 2018

Time of Day   Page 1

The Moons for 2018   Page 1

The S.A.D. Index   Page 2

The Almanack Weather   Page 2

Guide to Activity of Creatures   Page 3

Gardening with the Moon   Page 4

The Calendar of Feast Days   Page 4

The Almanack Daybook   Page 5

Almanack Essays by Bill Felker   Page 5

Index: Essays by Bill Felker   Page 5

Almanack Literature   Page 6

Index: Reader Stories   Page 7

The Monthly *Almanack* Sections Contain:

Seasonal Quotation
Gregorian Calendar
Essay by Bill Felker
Phases of the Moon
Meteorology: Cold Fronts and Lunar Influence
The Seasonal Affective Disorder Index
Astronomical Data: The Sun, The Planets,
The Stars, The Shooting Stars
Peak Activity Times for Creatures
Calendar of Feast Days for Gardeners and Homesteaders
The Almanack Daybook
Almanack Literature: A Reader Story

The Months of the Year

January	Page 9
February	Page 24
March	Page 37
April	Page 51
May	Page 66
June	Page 80
July	Page 92
August	Page 105
September	Page 118
October	Page 132
November	Page 144
December	Page 158
Valediction for the Year	Page 170
About Bill Felker	Page 171

Introductions
to Using *Poor Will's Almanack*

The Time of Day
In *Poor Will's Almanack*

All times in this *Almanack* are given in Eastern Standard Time.

The Moons for 2018

The following moon names used in *Poor Will's Almanack* correspond to events related to seasonal change. The days listed are for the new moon of each month.

December 18 of 2017: The Bedding Plant Moon
January 17: The Frolicking Fox Moon
February 15: The Ducks-Scouting-for-Nests Moon
March 17: The Golding Goldfinch Moon
April 16: The Termite Swarming Moon
May 15: The Daddy Longlegs Moon
June 13: The Turtle Hatching Moon
July 13: The Black-Eyed Susan Moon
August 11: The Blackberry Jam Moon
September 9: The Jumping Jumpseed Moon
October 9: The Shattering Ginkgo Moon
November 7: The Starling Murmuration Moon
December 7: The Flowering Jessamine Moon

About the Seasonal Affective Disorder (S.A.D.) Stress Index

The S.A.D. Stress Index measures the natural phenomena which are assumed to be related to S.A.D.—the day's length, the percentage of probable sunlight, the weather and the phase of the moon.

In order to create the Index, each of those factors was given a value from zero to 25, and then the four values were combined onto a scale of one to 100. Interpretation is simple: the higher the number, the greater the stress.

Lunar phase and proximity to Earth produce the most dramatic swings in the Index. For example, full moon days receive a rating of 25 and new moon days receive a 20, whereas days on which the moon enters its second and fourth quarters are given a rating of zero. Ratings are based on tidal and sociological information that suggests the moon is most influential when it is full, second-most influential when it is new and least influential at entry to its second and fourth phases.

Index readings are most useful in combination with a record of your own moods. Reference to the Index when you feel out of sorts may be a way of getting a feel for how seasonal affective disorder influences your life.

The Almanack Weather

The weather estimates in this *Almanack* are based on my charts of fractal weather patterns made between 1978 and 2017. Readers of my weekly and monthly columns throughout the United States have used these estimates successfully since 1984.

Poor Will's Almanack for 2018 integrates lunar conditions with brief descriptions of these weather systems in its "Almanack Daybook," noting how the moon's phase and proximity to Earth could influence frontal behavior.

A Guide to Activity of Creatures

The "Peak Activity Times for Creatures" section of each monthly section of the *Almanack* is a guide to lunar position and corresponding behavior.

Many people find that livestock, children, fish and game are more active (and dieting is more difficult) when the moon is overhead: at midday when the moon is new, in the afternoon and evening when the moon is in its first quarter, at night when the moon is full and in its third quarter, in the morning when the moon is in its fourth quarter. Second-best lunar times occur when the moon is below your location, 12 hours before or after those times noted above.

The approach of weather systems (high-pressure systems typically preceded by low-pressure systems) also influences fish and animal activity.

Farming and Gardening with the Moon

In general, planting crops that bear their fruit above the ground is recommended when the moon is waxing. Plant root crops, flower bulbs, trees and shrubs to promote root growth when the moon is waning.

According to a number of studies, the moon exerts less influence on ocean tides and on human and animal behavior when it comes into its second and fourth quarters. Therefore, it might make more sense to perform routine maintenance on your flock or herd near the date on which the moon enters its second or fourth quarter. On the other hand, tidal lunar influences have been proven to be greater at full moon and new moon times. You might expect more trouble with your animals, therefore, on or about new moon and full moon.

Livestock care should be less difficult during the relatively stable times between frontal systems listed in each month's meteorology section.

The Calendar of Feast Days

In this section, the *Almanack* lists the days of the year on which farmers, gardeners and homesteaders might expect the public to have increased interest in their livestock or produce. This calendar is also useful when one is planning strategies for marketing to particular ethnic or religious groups.

The Almanack Daybook

The daybook section of *Poor Will's Almanack for 2018* includes pivotal dates for the arrival of high-pressure systems, with comments on the effect of the moon on those systems. It also includes gardening and farming notes, as well as phenological information about changes in foliage, flowering and migratory activity throughout the year. Unless otherwise noted, "Daybook" notes refer to conditions in the East and Lower Midwest, especially along the 40th Parallel.

Almanack Essays by Bill Felker

The essays that appear on the first page of each month are taken from a nature column I have written for the *Yellow Springs News* since 1984.

Index of Essays by Bill Felker

Find these essays on the *first* page of each month.

January: *Buttercup, the Weather Dog*
February: *The Collapse of Winter*
March: *Notes from a Pilgrimage on the* Camino de
    Santiago
April: *Litany in Middle Spring*
May: *The Hinge of Early Summer*
A Note on Planting Beans
June: *Spiders*
July: *Counting Lilies*
August: *A Zillion Days*

September: *Inventory in Early Autumn*
October: *Bearing Witness*
November: *Hiding Under the Starling Murmuration
Moon*
December: *A Wreath for Spring*

Almanack Literature

Poor Will's readers have been contributing to his weekly and monthly columns since 1985. People have submitted memory stories, outhouse tales, narratives about unusual occurrences and special animals.

I include my favorite stories of recent years in each annual version of the *Almanack*. And you, reader, are invited to contribute! Payment for any story printed in the *Almanack* is five dollars. Send your tales to Poor Will, P.O. Box 431, Yellow Springs, OH 45387.

Index of Almanack Literature
Stories by Readers
of *Poor Will's Almanack*

Find these stories by going to the *last* page of each month.

January: *Political Unrest,* Mike Beard, Shelby,
    Ohio
February: *Whoosh!* By Dee Krieg, Seattle,
    Washington
March: *Dancing Pants* by Mrs. Oliver Gonzalez,
    Columbus, Ohio

April: *A Terrible Outhouse Afternoon* by Willy
    O'Holleran, Cincinnati, Ohio
May: *Blue Racers Can Kill!* By Anna Monroe
    Bruce, Fairborn, Ohio
June: *Surprise in the Outhouse* by Aldon Cisco,
    Waverly, Ohio
July: *A Rat in the Outhouse* by the Bylers,
    Greenwich, Ohio
August: *Love Before Cell Phones* by Eleanor
    Gnandt, Wellington, Ohio
September: *Nanny and the Lamb* by Bob, Bonnie
    and Shirley Applegate, Washington, Iowa
October: *Duck Killer* by Susan Perkins, Hardtimes
    Farm, Kentucky
November: *My Hero, My First Love* by Eunice
    Hicks, Willard, Ohio
December: "*It Takes a Village to Raise a Calf*" by
    E. Bridgewater, Scottsburg, India

JANUARY
2018

The smallest foothold on the surface of the globe places us in contact with the whole world's unending web of life. There are no isolated fragments. There are only threads and links and segments. Nothing is alone, nothing is unrelated, all are linked together.

Edwin Way Teale

The Gregorian Calendar

S	M	T	W	T	F	S
	1	2	3	4	5	6
7	8	9	10	11	12	13
14	15	16	17	18	19	20
21	22	23	24	25	26	27
28	29	30	31			

Buttercup, The Weather Dog

"Sine dubio canis speculum domini est."
(There is no doubt that a dog is the mirror of its
master.)
Celtus c940 AD

Several years ago, during a period of empty-nest anguish and remarkably bad judgment, my family purchased an overpriced English bulldog from one of the local mall pet stores. Buttercup was a sweet and lovable puppy, no doubt about it. But of her peculiar gifts I had no real notion until she matured a little.

Buttercup was certainly more intelligent than I. Having spent all of her life in a cage, she was reluctant to move a lot, and so she quickly trained me to carry her to the yard. I continued this for a year or so until I began to suspect she might be manipulating me.

Of course Buttercup did not like to go for walks. For the first nine months of her life, I practically had to drag her down the sidewalk if I wanted her to get some exercise. I was too astute to actually carry her on her walks, although once I did bring her home in my arms when she got overtired.

Buttercup had a number of fears. For one, she was afraid of her food dish, and she only ate if her meal was placed on a newspaper. I was the object of family ridicule for feeding Buttercup this way until a local trainer found out what I was doing.

"If you put the food in the dish and leave it there," she said, "the dog will eat."

So I followed her advice, and, indeed, after two days of pouting, Buttercup overcame her bowl phobia and ate like a normal dog (albeit with resentment and suspicion).

As with all of us, Buttercup's deepest psychological wounds were the source of her greatest gifts and insights. One of her wounds was a fear of noise. When trucks went by as we walked down the street, she trembled and tried to pull away. No matter how many trucks she was exposed to, she always reacted the same way.

As a puppy she would beg to be held during storms, and we indulged her, of course. She would shiver and shake until the weather passed, then be all right again. When she grew older, however, her emotions would sometimes get out of hand.

By the time she was two years old, she had started chewing on things at the height of her fear. She ate the back door, a nice set of French doors we had recently refinished, our bedroom door, a louvered door which led to the laundry room, and a computer printer cable.

Once she attacked a utility closet and ripped apart a full bag of mortar mix, emerging with her mouth full of cement, and cement dust all over her eyes. Luckily, with veterinary help, she suffered no lasting damage. Not that the doctors have been all that helpful. One vet suggested using tough love to discourage her outbursts. That didn't work. A different specialist recommended desensitization with thunderstorm tapes. We were afraid to try that. Medication was only partially effective.

Disturbed by her pain and having only limited success in finding help, we took longer than we should have to notice her true gift, her ability to forecast the weather. Indeed, Buttercup could foretell the coming of violent meteorological conditions long before they arrived at our house on High Street. I was often startled in the middle of summer nights to hear her pacing with fear. By morning, the lightning would strike nearby. Even when the sun was shining at dawn, if Buttercup was panting, I could be sure that rain would fall that day.

Comparing Buttercup's forecasts to those of the Doppler radar, I found that she was able to sense the approach of a storm 50 to 100 miles away, and she began hyperventilating even before the barometer began to drop. Tranquilizers didn't seem to dull her sensitivity in the slightest; even though they helped her not to eat the remaining doors in the house, they left her the gift of prophecy. I knew that she could still tell the future, even under sedation. I would see it in her eyes.

As to whether her special powers were due to chronic arthritis, to exceptionally acute hearing, to lunar phases, to shifts in atmospheric pressure or to psychic ability, I and her veterinarians could never decide. I do suspect, however, that she and I (both of us too influenced by the moon and weather) were locked in a terrible codependency, the kind Celtus spoke of when he said: *Canis speculum domini est.*

The Phases of the Bedding Plant Moon and the Frolicking Fox Moon

As the bedding plants of 2018 sprout in the safety of their warm grow-lights, the parallel world of Deep Winter is no less active, no matter the cold. Even though January temperatures are the lowest of the year, foxes and coyotes come out in the night to play and mate; owls seek nesting sites. Under the milder nights of the Frolicking Fox Moon, skunks emerge from their dens to look for love, and sometimes salamanders come together in the warmest slime.

January 1: The Bedding Plant Moon is full at 9:24 p.m. and it reaches perigee at 6:54 p.m. When full moon occurs on the same date as perigee, it is often called a "Supermoon."

January 8: The moon enters its final quarter at 5:25 p.m.

January 14: The moon reaches apogee at 9:10 p.m.

January 16: The Frolicking Fox Moon is new at 9:17 p.m.

January 23: The moon enters its second quarter at 9:26 p.m.

January 30: The moon reaches perigee at 4:54 a.m.

January 31: The moon is full at 8:26 a.m. This moon is a "Blue Moon," the second full moon in the same month and the second "Supermoon."

A total eclipse of the moon will occur in the morning of the 31st, but it will only be completely visible in Hawaii, Alaska and western Canada. On the other hand, it will be partially visible at moonset throughout most of the continental United States.

Meteorology

High-pressure systems are due to cross the country on or around the following dates: January 1, 5, 10, 15, 19, 25, 31. If strong storms occur this month, weather patterns suggest that they will happen during the following periods: January 1-2, 8-12 and 19-24 (the transition time to Late Winter).

New moon on January 16 and full moon on January 1 and 31 are likely to intensify the weather systems due around those dates. The coldest January days usually fall between the 7th and the 10th, as well as between the 15th and the 18th.

The S.A.D. Index

January brings the year's coldest weather to every state of the Union, and seasonal affective disorder is more frequent this month than at any time during the winter. Since meteorological conditions are relatively stable, only the moon's phase causes significant increases and decreases in the intensity of S.A.D.

Key for Interpreting the S.A.D. Index:
Totals of 100 to 80: Severe stress
79 to 55: Severe to moderate stress
54 to 40: Moderate stress
39 to 25: Light to moderate stress
24 and below: Light stress

Day	Clouds	Weather	Day	Moon	Totals
January 1:	25	24	25	25	99
January 8:	25	25	24	0	74
January 16:	25	25	24	15	89
January 23:	25	23	23	0	71
January 31:	25	22	22	25	94

The Sun

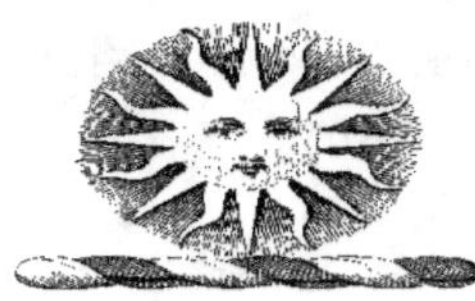

Perihelion, the point at which the Earth and the Sun are closest to one another, occurs on January 3 at 2:12 a.m. The Sun enters the Late Winter constellation of Aquarius on January 20.

The Planets

Find Jupiter and Mars in the southeast before dawn, together in boxy Libra. Saturn follows both Jupiter and Mars in Sagittarius close to sunrise. Venus is not visible this month. A star chart will show you the location of both Libra and Sagittarius, helping you to locate the planets

The Stars

Follow Orion during the first months of the year to track the progress of the season. In Deep Winter's January, Orion's giant figure fills the southern sky at 11:00 p.m. To his right, the red eye of Taurus (the star Aldebaran) leads the way. Behind him comes Canis Minor and its brightest star, Procyon.

The Shooting Stars

January's shooting stars are the Quadrantids; they appear early in the first week of the month, most heavily on January 3 and 4, at the rate of about 35 per hour. Look for them after midnight in the eastern sky near Arcturus.

Peak Activity Times for Creatures

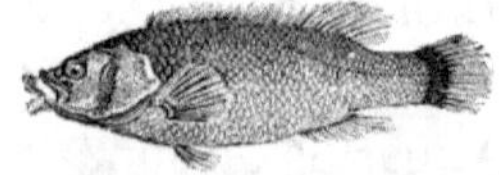

The following guide to lunar position shows when the moon is above (Best times) or below (Second-best times) the country, and, therefore, the period during which livestock, people, fish and game are typically the most active and the hungriest.

Date	Best	Second-Best
January 1 – 7:	Midnight to Dawn	Afternoons

January 8 – 15 :   Mornings   Evenings
January 16 – 22 :   Afternoon   Midnight to Dawn
January 23 – 31:   Evenings   Mornings

Calendar of Feast Days and Holidays for Farmers, Gardeners and Homesteaders

January 6, 2018: Epiphany (Three-Kings Day): Many Christians celebrate this feast with a fine meal and religious services. Milk-fed lambs are often in demand for this market.

January 13, 2018: The pre-Lenten carnival season begins near this date, one month before Mardi Gras. Explore marketing lambs for cookouts during this period.

The Almanack Daybook
for January of 2018

1: Today is the first day of Deep Winter, the coldest season of the year. Full moon and perigee (creating a "Supermoon") are likely to intensify the first high-pressure system of January. Expect precipitation on New Year's Eve with severe weather to follow.

2: Pruning is recommended for the next two weeks as the moon wanes. Spray your broad-leafed evergreens with anti-drying agents to prevent winterkill. Then take cuttings to propagate shrubs, trees and houseplants.

3: Even though the Sun reaches perihelion today (its position closest to Earth), the harshest period of the year has begun. Between now and the end of the month, average temperatures are the coldest of the year.

4: As the barometer falls in advance of tomorrow's cold wave, seeds should be especially eager to sprout, and fish and game should become more active and increase feeding.

5: If you are planning surgery or dental work for this month, consider scheduling it before the new moon on the 16th

6: Pines have started to pollinate, and allergy season begins. In the greenhouse, the season of jade tree bloom ends as camellia time spreads in the Deep South and black bears end hibernation in Southern forests.

7: Today is the Christian feast of the Epiphany. If you have made a twelve-week "Advent" wreath, today marks the end of the fifth week. When the twelfth week is over, the chilly but promising season of Early Spring will have begun.

8: Today is Plough Monday, the traditional beginning of the farm and garden year. In the week ahead, continue to put in bedding plant seeds as the moon darkens. And the best lunar times to work with your livestock are around the time the moon enters its fourth phase (today) and its second phase (on the 23rd).

9: The moon's weak position should soften the January 10 weather system. Across the South, put in the hardy vegetable garden for Early Spring.

10: Today is the average date for the year's third major cold front.

11: The main lambing and kidding season begins as January progresses. More lambs and kids are born in the next eight weeks than in any other months.

12: Farm and garden seeds normally reach retail outlets by today, and florists and grocery stores display spring daffodils, crocus and tulips.

13: Between the middle of January through the middle of May, spring moves from New Orleans at a rate of about five miles per day or one degree Fahrenheit every four to five days.

14: Today's lunar apogee may increase the likelihood for precipitation in front of the January 15 front.

15: Tomorrow's new moon is likely to strengthen the cold front due to cross the Mississippi near that date.

16: Throughout the South, sap should start to run in maples as the moon waxes. Yellow sow thistles blossom in the Carolinas. White clover, red clover and dandelions are in full bloom in Florida, and the squat winter thistles are fat and thick there.

17: Dependable companions in the cold winter mornings, crows now become more boisterous; their migration typically starts near this date.

18: Frost seeding typically begins at this time of the year. Broadcast crops such as red clover in the pastures, and scatter grass seed over bare spots on the lawn. The freezing and thawing of the ground works the seeds into the ground.

19: The January Thaw period begins around this date and often lasts through the 25th.

20: In the South, pasture season can be underway by now, and fields are starting to turn a deeper green.

21: Opossums and raccoons become more active at night as Deep Winter wanes.

22: Seasonal markers now include the beginning of cardinal mating songs before dawn, the appearance of the first snowdrop, day lily, crocus, daffodil and peony foliage (and maybe a bud or flower), the rapid disappearance of the remaining orange euonymus berries and the last seeds of the small-flowered asters.

23: The moon, entering its mild second quarter today, increases the chances of a significant thaw.

24: By the end of the week, the first large waves of robins and bluebirds cross the Ohio River.

25: The cold front due near this date often puts an abrupt end to chances for a January thaw. Secondary frontal conditions, sometimes carrying moist Gulf air, can set off powerful blizzards around the 27th.

26: Today is the first day of the season of Late Winter. This season contains five to six major cold fronts and lasts from January 26 through February 18. Although this period can be one of the coldest of the year in the North, its thaws accelerate the swelling of buds and the blooming of early bulbs.

27: Throughout the country, average temperatures, which had remained stable from the middle of January, climb one degree.

28: Full moon on the 30th increases the chances for seasonal affective disorders.

29: Along the Gulf coast, elderberries and azaleas bloom; new calves are out in the fields and turtles hatch.

30: Today's lunar perigee combines with

tomorrow's full "Supermoon" to create a strong likelihood of heavy precipitation, followed by severe cold.

31: The sun's declination passes 17 degrees 31 minutes today, one quarter of the way to spring equinox, just as the final weather system of January arrives under the frigid influence of the full moon.

Almanack Literature
Political Unrest
By Mike Beard, Shelby, Ohio

This story goes back a few years; as a matter of fact, it goes back to 1960 during another political campaign. As most of you remember, the presidency of the United States was being sought by Jack Kennedy and Richard Nixon. I was in high school and lived on a small farm in northwest Ohio. The political hype was at its greatest all year.

I raised sheep on the farm at that time, and in January I had purchased two beautiful Hampshire rams to be used for breeding services. These rams were my pride and joy, and they were pampered and given the best of living conditions in the barn. They together shared a large horse stall. Both being as pampered as they were needed names, so one was called Kennedy and the other Nixon.

As the political climate grew, so did the rams. By September, it was breeding season, and they were turned into pasture with the ewes for breeding. As rams will do, they became aggressive, not just with themselves, but with humans…mainly myself.

You could not turn your back on either one of them or you would get butted rather hard. While bending over mending fences one day, Nixon head-butted me, knocked me on my butt and gave me a mild concussion. So needless to say, after that point, I was never able to trust them again. I still loved them, but after that I was careful and always had an eye on them when I went to the barn to do chores.

Sometime in late October, I segregated them from the rest of the sheep, and they were back in their shared stall. I noticed that they would have head butting contests, and it appeared to be getting worse. I decided they had to be separated from each other as they would butt heads relentlessly. I put a substantial gate between them to solve the head-butting problem, or so I thought.

Two days before the 1960 presidential election between Jack Kennedy and Richard Nixon, I went to the barn to do chores and found both of my much-loved Hampshire rams dead. They had torn down the gate between them and fought until they broke each others' necks and died.

At that time, my father said, "That was a bad omen!" And I guess history tells us he was right.

FEBRUARY
2018

No winter lasts forever; no spring skips its turn.

Hal Borland

The Gregorian Calendar

S	M	T	W	T	F	S
				1	2	3
4	5	6	7	8	9	10
11	12	13	14	15	16	17
18	19	20	21	22	23	24
25	26	27	28			

The Collapse of Winter

The flowering season has just barely begun in the warmest corners of the Lower Midwest, and one might take an early stock of the landscape before momentum builds much more.

The exact end of winter comes well before the major thaws, arriving unseen in the coldest weeks of the year when the March and April bulbs follow their own subterranean schedules and push up through mulch beneath the snow.

Walking through your neighborhood, you might

find evidence of that movement, find that some daffodil stalks have reached two inches high, and that a few tulips and hyacinths are up at least an inch. Snowdrops and aconite may be ready to bloom. Lilac buds are swollen, fat green and gold. On the pussy willow branches, a few catkins are cracking. Garlic mustard, wild mallow and henbit are growing new leaves. Chickweed is spreading quickly. Wild strawberry, celandine, wild onions, hollyhocks, sweet William, lamb's ear, lungwort, dandelion, motherwort, and great mullein have remained intact through January and are waiting for a little more sun.

Spring, of course, is as much a state of mind as a state of nature. The end of winter always appears in the eye of the beholder. Critical mass for the arrival of spring rests less on the total quantity of observations than on one crucial scent or sight or sound that tips the scales of private time. Each person encounters that pivotal event at a different moment and in a different way. And whenever that one event occurs, then the entire scaffolding of the old year collapses, and all the pieces of the new year take on meaning as they fall into place.

Phases of the Frolicking Fox Moon and the Ducks-Scouting-for-Nests Moon

As Deep Winter comes to a close, ducks and geese begin scouting for nesting sites along the shores of rivers and lakes. Parallel events in the Ducks-Scouting-for-Nests Moon are the running of maple sap, the movement of the first wave of robins from the South, the calling of doves before dawn, the cracking of pussy willows, the emergence of snowdrops and snow crocus in dooryard gardens and the blossoming of snow trillium in the bottomlands.

February 7: The Frolicking Fox Moon enters its final phase at 10:54 a.m.
February 11: The moon reaches apogee at 9:16 a.m.
February 15: The Ducks-Scouting-for-Nests Moon is new at 4:05 p.m.
February 23: The moon enters its second quarter at 3:09 a.m.
February 27: The moon reaches perigee at 9:48 a.m.

Note: There is no full moon this February.

Meteorology

Significant cold waves are due to cross the United States around the following dates: February 3, 6, 11, 15, 20, 24 and 27.

If strong storms occur this month, they will be most likely to strike on or around February 2-4, 6-9, 14-18 and 24-27.

New moon on February 15 and lunar perigee on February 27 are likely to increase the intensity of the weather systems that typically arrive near those dates.

The S.A.D. Stress Index

The likelihood of seasonal stress begins to fall steadily throughout February. Even though clouds usually continue to deprive the human brain of the benefits of sunlight, the length of the day complements the slowly improving temperatures, and the S.A.D. Index dips more frequently into the moderate (but still troubling) 50s and 60s when the moon lies in its weaker phases.

Key for Interpreting the S.A.D. Index:
Totals of 100 to 80: Severe stress
79 to 55: Severe to moderate stress

54 to 40: Moderate stress
39 to 25: Light to moderate stress
24 and below: Light stress

Day	Clouds	Weather	Day	Moon	Totals
February 1:	25	20	22	24	91
February 7:	23	24	20	0	67
February 15:	22	20	18	15	75
February 23:	22	19	18	0	59
February 27:	22	18	17	24	81

The Sun

A partial eclipse of the sun will occur February 15, but it will only be visible in the Southern Hemisphere. On February 18, the Sun reaches halfway to equinox. This landmark in the solar year is called Cross-Quarter Day. On February 19, the Sun enters the Early Spring constellation of Pisces.

The Planets

♃ ♄ ♂ ♀

Rising after midnight, Jupiter remains in Libra, preceding Mars, which moves to Ophiuchus. Both planets are visible before dawn in the southeast, followed by Saturn. Venus is not visible this month.

The Stars

Around midnight in February, Orion dominates the southwestern sky in his Early Spring position. Almost directly overhead are the twin stars of Gemini, Castor and Pollux, followed by the constellation Cancer (that looks a little like a person walking).

Peak Activity Times for Creatures

The following guide to lunar position shows when the moon is above (Best times) or below (Second-best times) the country, and, therefore, the period during which livestock, people, fish and game are typically the most active and the hungriest.

Date	Best	Second-Best
February 1 – 6:	Midnight to Dawn	Afternoons
February 7 – 14:	Mornings	Evenings
February 15 – 22:	Afternoons	Midnight to Daw
February 23 – 28:	Evenings	Mornings

Calendar of Feast Days and Holidays for Farmers, Gardeners and Homesteaders

February 13, 2018: Mardi Gras: The month-long carnival season ends today. The 14th is Ash Wednesday and the start of the Lenten fast.

February 16, 2018: Tet, Vietnamese New Year and Chinese New Year (the Year of the Dog): The Chinese market is often strong throughout the winter, favoring sheep (but not dogs!) in the 70-pound live-weight range.

February 27, 2018: Dominican Republic Independence Day: Areas that have a sizeable population of residents from the Dominican Republic may show an increase in sales of lambs and kids that weigh between 20 to 35 pounds.

The Almanack Daybook for February of 2018

1: As the moon wanes through its third quarter, most mid-winter abortions often occur in livestock. While the moon darkens, plant bulbs, shrubs and trees throughout the southern half of the United States. Continue frost seeding of pastures and seeding of bedding plants and hardy vegetables in the North.

2: Today is Groundhog Day. This year, the strong lunar position at the end of January is likely to delay or negate the Groundhog Day Thaw that often characterizes the early days of February. On the other hand, six weeks from today, the hardiest of spring cabbages and kales can be set out in most gardens below the 40th Parallel.

3: February 3 is one of the February days most likely to bring dangerous storms to the Plains and tornadoes to the South.

Schedule routine livestock maintenance and foot clipping before new moon (on the 15th). Clip your fingernails in preparation for lambing and kidding.

4: The pollen season, which began with the pollination of pine trees, now intensifies across the South with the blooming of mountain cedar, acacia, smooth alder, bald cypress, American elm, red maple, white poplar and black willow. Bluegrass, which stopped flowering in midsummer, revives and starts its seeding cycle. When warm Gulf winds bring thaws across the North, all this pollen comes along, too.

5: The weakening moon should moderate the temperatures in this month's first two weeks, softening the cold fronts of the 6th and the 11th.

6: Cardinals now sing all day. In northern Mexico, the remaining monarch butterflies are moving toward the Texas border. They will reach the Gulf coast in small groups during mid to late March, and their offspring will find the Northern states in May.

7: Bees come looking for skunk cabbage when temperatures warm to 50 degrees. Deer gather throughout the month to feed in herds. Turkeys are flocking now; they will disband and scatter into smaller family groups by April.

8: Prepare for possible drought by making sure your soil has sufficient potassium and phosphorus.

9: Doves begin mating calls before dawn, joining the titmice and the cardinals. Red-winged blackbirds migrate north to Midwestern wetlands.

10: Plant onions directly in the ground as soon as the soil is properly prepared.

11: Lunar apogee today should help make livestock maintenance and child care slightly less difficult. It may also weaken the February 11 cold front.

12: The pace of spring quickens as the sun reaches 40 percent of the way to equinox today. Continue planting and frost seeding throughout the period. Under the dark moon, spray trees with dormant oil when temperatures rise into the upper 30s or 40s. In garden ponds, algae is growing thicker, a sign that thaws accumulate in water as well as in the soil.

13: All along the Gulf of Mexico, violets are coming into full bloom, along with wintersweet, winter honeysuckle, Lenten-rose and Jessamine. Strawberries often have new foliage in Tennessee; in Florida, the strawberries are turning red.

14: Prepare landscaping, garden and field maps, including plans for double cropping, intercropping and companion planting. The following vegetables can be planted a month before your last frost: peas, lettuce, spinach, cabbage, collards, kale, onions, potatoes and radishes.

15: The cold front that arrives in the middle of February is often followed by slightly milder temperatures and Early Spring. Today's new moon, however, is likely to delay the arrival of that season. A few markers of the six-week season of Early Spring: the sporadic blooming of dandelions in sunnier lawns, the increasing activity of water striders and small moths on warmer days, the running of maple sap (as new moon and Early Spring arrive together), the nesting of cardinals, the nighttime mating of salamanders in shallow pools, the courtship of raccoons. And bald eagles incubate their eggs at this time.

16: As the moon weakens and comes into its second quarter on February 23, it should temper the February 20 and 24 cold fronts and favor the start of sapping time. When the temperature reaches 55 degrees, then open up your beehives and check to see that the bees are alive and well. If you find eggs in the cells, you know the queen has not died.

17: Throughout the central states, the ground temperature is moving above 35 degrees, the temperature at which earthworms become active. That means the pastures are starting to grow again.

18: Today is Cross-Quarter Day, the first day of Early Spring. Although the weather is usually raw, the first trees and flowers bloom and migratory activity increases. A return of colder weather between the 24th and March 7 typically delays the rapid development of spring flowers.

19: In the Southwest, wildflowers bloom across the deserts if there has been enough rain.

20: The weak moon today is expected to lighten the February 20 cold front. Red and silver maples bloom at lower elevations in the Appalachians, introducing welcome color to the Early Spring landscape as well as offering pollen for early bees.

21: The passage of the February 20th cold front marks the end of the snowiest part of the year in most states.

22: By this week of the year, the beginnings of snowdrop season, aconite season, crocus season, and daffodil budding season are all a part of the natural history record throughout the lower two-thirds of the United States

23: In the Southwest, put in the last of the potato crop. Cut the Arizona hay as the moon wanes.

24: The cold front due to arrive in the nation's midsection within a few days of the 24th brings "Snowdrop Winter" to the land.

25: Bee season has begun in the Deep South. Honeybees and carpenter bees collect pollen from dandelions, yellow-flowered wild radishes, red maples, henbit, blue toadflax, white clover and chickweed.

26: As February ends cows, heifers and bulls are wormed before they are turned out to pasture. Mares show signs of estrus as the days grow longer. Chipmunks come out to play and mate in the sun.

27: Lunar perigee today, combined with full moon on March 1, should pull the maple sap into pails throughout much of the country. Redbuds and azaleas are in full bloom in Georgia, rhododendrons just starting to come in. In the lowlands of Mississippi, swamp buttercups are open, violets and black medic, too.

28: With the powerful full moon on March 1, watch for late abortions in weak animals. This full moon is likely to bring blizzard conditions to the Great Plains and then all across the Midwest.

Almanack Literature
Whoosh!
By Dee Krieg, Seattle, Washington

"Into the car now," Grandpa ordered, and we piled into the old Oakland: Grandma, Mommy, Daddy, Great-aunt Lizzi, Auntie Sadie, Sissie and I on this star-studded night of August 1932. Five miles out of town at the Union Pacific railroad crossing, the streamliner called "City of Celina" would come roaring from the flatlands heading east.

Grandpa drove pretty fast, fifteen miles an hour, and we all sat quiet, expectant. Finally the crossing appeared. There were people lined up along the tracks, everyone looking toward the western horizon. We climbed out of the car, Mommy and Daddy holding on to us, and joined the crowds.

Suddenly everyone was quiet. We felt it before we saw it. The vibration in the ground was subtle at first, and then we could feel the rolling thunder underneath our leather soles. In the distance we saw a tiny bright eye glistening in that summer sky and we knew it was not a star.

Our muscles tensed. Mommy and Daddy grasped our hands tighter. Parents shouted to their kids to stand close. And the eye became brighter and brighter and suddenly a loud roaring noise eclipsed the night sky and the sleek, silvered body of the streamliner bore down upon us, the noise of the engine pulsating in our ears so that we pressed nearer to our parents, listening to the tracks singing their metallic siren song, and then it flashed past all of us, the crossing signals clanging their alarms and their red lights blinking.

And we stood transfixed, looking in at the lighted windows of the privileged sitting in their silver coaches, little children pressing their noses against the windows and waving at us, and we all waved and waved and waved until the last car vanished into the soft dark at the edge of our world.

MARCH
2018

*Afoot and light-hearted I take to the open road,
Healthy, free, the world before me,
The long brown path before me leading wherever I
choose.*

Walt Whitman

The Gregorian Calendar

S	M	T	W	T	F	S
				1	2	3
4	5	6	7	8	9	10
11	12	13	14	15	16	17
18	19	20	21	22	23	24
25	26	27	28	29	30	31

Notes from a Pilgrimage
on the *Camino de Santiago*, Galicia, Spain

Last March and April, I took a walk of more than a hundred miles across the landscape of spring on the *Camino de Santiago* in Spain.

The vegetation and the emerging leaves on the canopy above me offered many markers for the progress of the season as well as for my own progress along the path on which I averaged about seven to ten miles in a day.

I hiked down country roads and paths through farmland and eucalyptus forests, the sky clearest blue, no clouds mile after mile, sun warming my neck. All the time I was heading west toward what is called the "End of the World" in Finisterre, the last outcropping of Europe.

Along the *camino* were wild large yellow primroses, whispering streams of runoff from the succulent fields, waysides of violet and gold ground-cover bloom, grass so fresh, nothing around me old or dying, warbling birds all the way.

Hills were pale green with early leaves, pastures deep green, stone walls speckled with heavy moss, plums and apples in bloom. From the early afternoons toward evening, I saw so many butterflies: cabbage whites, sulfurs, blues, fritillaries, many in randori play and mating.

From home in Ohio, Jill sent photos of April: redbuds flowering, a few tulips out, blue spiderwort in bloom, one garden with daffodils and hyacinths. In many yards and gardens, northern Spain was a few weeks ahead of southwestern Ohio; I walked beside the future on my pilgrimage, and I arrived home in May to find where I had been.

Phases of the Ducks-Scouting-for-Nests Moon and the Golding Goldfinch Moon

When spring advances north from the Gulf of Mexico and ducks and geese are nesting, goldfinches gradually lose their winter color and become gold once again. Daffodils and golden goldfinches go together in the year, complemented by the full flowering of squills, croci, spring iris and early Lenten roses (hellebores) in time for Easter.

March 1: The Ducks-Scouting-for-Nests Moon is full at 8:51 p.m.

March 9: The moon enters its final quarter at 6:19 a.m.

March 11: The moon reaches apogee at 4:13 a.m.

March 17: The Golding Goldfinch Moon is new at 6:11 a.m.

March 24: The moon enters its second phase at 10:35 a.m.

March 26: The moon is at perigee at 12:17 p.m.

March 31: The moon is full at 7:36 a.m. This is the second Blue Moon of 2018

Meteorology

Major March weather systems usually cross the Mississippi River on March 2, 5 (usually the most severe front of the month), 9 (ordinarily followed by quite mild temperatures), 14, 19 (frequently the second-coldest front of March), 24 (often followed by the best weather so far in the year) and 29.

Major storms are most likely to occur on the days between March 9 and 14, between March 19 and 30. New moon on March 17 and full moon on the 1st and 31st are likely to bring frost deep into Southern gardens and increased chances of storms across the North.

The S.A.D. Stress Index

Cloud cover and inclement weather continue to hold Index readings relatively high during March. The day keeps lengthening, however, and improved meteorological conditions toward the end of the month push the Index numbers down into the middle 50s and 60s after equinox. As in previous months, lunar phase and proximity to Earth increase the likelihood that you may experience S.A.D.

Key for Interpreting the S.A.D. Index:
Totals of 100 to 80: Severe stress
79 to 55: Severe to moderate stress
54 to 40: Moderate stress
39 to 25: Light to moderate stress
24 and below: Light stress

Day	Clouds	Weather	Daylight	Moon	Totals
March 1:	21	18	17	25	81
March 9:	20	16	15	0	51
March 17:	18	13	14	20	65
March 25:	17	12	12	15	56
March 31:	16	11	11	25	63

The Sun

Equinox occurs at 11:15 a.m. March 20. The Sun enters the Middle Spring sign of Aries on March 21. *Daylight Saving Time begins at 2:00 a.m. on Sunday, March 11.*

The Planets

Now in Sagittarius with Saturn, Mars still lies in the southeast before the sun comes up. Jupiter, traveling along the southern horizon through the night, remains bright in Libra. Venus finally becomes visible for the first time this year as the evening star in Pisces.

The Stars

On March evenings, the constellation Leo, with its keystone star, Regulus, lie in the center of the sky. The Pleiades, followed by Taurus and its red eye, lead Orion into his Early Spring position in the far west. The Big Dipper is moving into the sky almost directly above you.

Peak Activity Times for Creatures

The following guide to lunar position shows when the moon is above (Best times) or below (Second-best times) the country, the periods during which livestock, people, fish and game are typically the most active and the hungriest.

Date	Best	Second-Best
March 1 – 8:	Midnight to Dawn	Afternoons
March 9 – 16:	Mornings	Evenings
March 17 – 23:	Afternoons	Midnight to Dawn
March 24 – 31:	Evenings	Mornings

Calendar of Feast Days and Holidays for Farmers, Gardeners and Homesteaders

March 30 – April 7, 2018: Passover: The Jewish market typically is best after religious holidays come to a close. Milk-fed lambs and kids below 60 pounds are favored for the Passover market. Lamb stew is a traditional Seder dish at Passover Seder dinners.

The Almanack Daybook
for March of 2018

1: The Ducks-Scouting-for-Nests Moon is full this evening, and full moon today so close to perigee (on February 27) creates lunar conditions that strengthen the first cold front of March, increasing the likelihood of snow in the North and tornadoes in the South.

Onions seeds and sets, potatoes, radishes, beets, carrots and turnips can be sown directly in the ground anytime between now and new moon on the 17th. All bedding plants should be started in their flats. Only eleven weeks remain before the most delicate flowers and vegetables can be planted outside in all but the northernmost states. Four weeks until most hardy plants can be set out.

2: Complete the spraying of fruit trees. Do late pruning on colder afternoons. Spread fertilizer after testing the soil. In lakes and rivers, walleye, sauger, saugeye, muskie, bass and crappie start spring feeding.

3: Worms cross sidewalks and parking lots in the rain, a sign that the ground has thawed well above 40 degrees.

4: Graft and repot houseplants. Dig fence post holes while the ground is soft and wet. Put in oats or ryegrass for quick vegetative cover. This is also a good time to seed and fertilize the lawn.

5: Precipitation and wind typically mark the high-pressure system that usually arrives on or about the

5th. The last or second-last major snowstorm of the first half of the year sometimes strikes the Middle Atlantic region today.

6: Winter juncos migrate north for breeding. Male red-winged blackbirds (that arrived about two weeks ago) sing in the swamps as females join them in their nesting areas.

7: Azaleas bloom all across the Deep South. In the East, buds lengthen and brighten on multiflora roses, honeysuckles, mock orange and lilacs. Forsythia blooms in Memphis.

8: Warm-weather crops like tomatoes should be ready to set out on the first of May if you start them under lights this week. Try cucumbers, peppers, eggplant, squash and all delicate herbs or flowers indoors.

9: The March 9 cold front is often the most dangerous and the coldest high-pressure system in the first two-thirds of March.

10: This is an early date for cherry trees to be in full bloom in Washington, D.C., and it is also the average date for flower and garden shows throughout the East. In the Northeast, the coats of snowshoe hares begin changing from white to brown. Throughout the Midwest and North, crows pair off and select nesting sites. Purple martins migrate. Peregrine falcons lay their eggs. Bald eagle chicks hatch. White tundra swans usually land along Lake Erie. Along the 40th Parallel, lawn growth is usually perceptible now, three weeks before grass is ready to cut.

11: Today's lunar apogee will decrease the likelihood of storms after the March 9 weather system (but not before) and stimulate warmer temperatures. Mites, scale and aphid eggs mature quickly on fruit trees if the temperature climbs above 60 degrees. The insects will be more easily controlled by dormant oil spray the closer they are to hatching.

Honeysuckle leaves are often opening now, one of the first steps in the greening of the undergrowth. Parsnip, horseradish, dock and dandelion roots can be dug at this time as foliage just begins to emerge; root quality is usually at its best before the soil begins to warm. Set out flats of pansies on milder afternoons

12: This is the week that the first mosquito bites and that the box elders and silver maples come into bloom in the Lower Midwest.

13: The front that often arrives near this date is expected to be strengthened by the upcoming new moon on the 17th.

14: Foliage of yarrow, lupine, phlox, columbine, coneflower, yarrow, sage, sweet pea, mallow, wild parsnip, goldenrod, snow-on-the mountain, New England aster, Queen Anne's lace, pyrethrum, bleeding heart, lamb's quarters and evening primrose is coming up across the land.

15: Midseason crocus plants bloom beside the

earlier snow crocus. Cardinals now sing a quarter of an hour earlier than they did two weeks ago.

16: The mass flowering of violets and dandelions now occurs in the South and will arrive in the Lower Midwest in three or four weeks. Water striders breed in the ponds and rivers. Mock orange leafs out beside the new honeysuckle foliage. Nine weeks until tender vegetables can be set out.

17: Today's new moon not only brings robins into song across most of the nation, it offers some of the very best lunar seed starting of the entire year for flowers and for vegetables that will produce their fruit above the ground. And today is St. Patrick's Day, a traditional time to plant peas and potatoes. In the wetlands, ragwort buds when weeping willows glow yellow-green. In the woods, toad trillium pushes up through the leaves as turkeys start to gobble.

18: Clean and disinfect the henhouse as spring turns to summer. Fertilize your pastures several weeks before you let your livestock graze. Keep an eye out for bloat, however, as you let your kids, calves and lambs enjoy the new greenery.

19: Beginning today and lasting through the 30th, the second major March storm period increases the threat of tornadoes in the South and surprise blizzards in the North. The season of flowering fruit trees is underway through the South. May apples emerge below the Mason-Dixon Line, morel mushrooms soon to follow.

20: Today is equinox, and the front closest to equinox historically brings freezing temperatures and clear skies to the northern half of the nation. In spite of the chill, the *cornus mas* shrubs come into full bloom, their golden flowers foreshadowing the forsythia that will blossom by the end of the month. Now begin your spring wildflower walks: snow trillium is blossoming, and violet cress is budding.

21: Clematis leaves emerge throughout the Lower Midwest. Comfrey leaves reach two inches long. Motherwort swells into clumps, and henbit is in full bloom. Daffodils and magnolias blossom in Cincinnati. Sandhill cranes migrate in the Rocky Mountains.

22: When new raspberry leaves are almost ready for tea, scillas color city lawns blue, and soft touch-me-nots have sprouted in the wetlands. Frosts could be over for the winter along the 40th Parallel, but an average year brings about twenty more to Northern gardens.

23: Transplant shade and fruit trees, shrubs, grape vines, strawberries, raspberries and roses while the ground temperature remains in the 40s and 50s. Complete field and garden planting preparations.

24: The moon enters its second phase at 10:35 a.m., and the March 24 weather system should be relatively mild under this weak lunar period. This is the time of year that Early Spring's first butterflies—the question marks, the mourning cloaks, the tortoise shells and the cabbage whites—

typically emerge along the 40th parallel.

25: Violet cress flowers in the bottomlands. Chickweed and shepherd's purse are open in the alleys. The first white star magnolia blossoms unravel in town.

26: The moon is at perigee this afternoon, strengthening as it continues to wax gibbous.

27: In wilderness areas of the Southwest, late March often brings the peak of wildflower season.

28: Bloodroot opens in parklands when forsythia flowers in town. Ragweed sprouts, and cardinals now sing 45 minutes earlier than they sang four weeks ago.

29: The last front of March (influenced by proximity to lunar perigee and full moon) arrives near this date

30: Along the 40th Parallel, today marks the arrival of Middle Spring, a four-week period during which almost all the field crops are planted and gardeners set out onion sets, broccoli, cabbage, collards and kale.

31: The moon is full this morning. This is the second full moon of March and the second Blue Moon of 2018.

Almanack Literature
Dancing Pants
By Mrs. Oliver Gonzalez, Columbus, Ohio

Well, it was a hot day, one of those days this past July when people were threatened by the heat. Our electric dryer was broken, and I had a whole basket of wet laundry to deal with.

Luckily, we had two apple trees in the back yard about thirty feet apart. I went down to the hardware store and bought some clothesline rope and strung a makeshift drying apparatus between the apple trees. Then I hung out as many of my clothes as would fit, including two pairs of my husband's jeans.

And then, with making supper and trying to figure out where the kids went, I forgot about everything on the line. And it got dark, the moon came up, and we all went to bed and fell asleep.

Then about four in the morning, our two mutt dogs started to carry on, barking and jumping at the back door trying to get out. My husband rolled over and hit at the alarm clock, as though that would quiet things down, and I got up and went out to see what was going on.

Lo and behold, I could see all the clothes dancing in the bright moonlight, with two pairs of jeans dancing and jumping up and down a lot harder than the rest.

I shouldn't have opened the back door, but I was half asleep and I did it.

Wham, the dogs burst through the screen, leapt off the porch and went at the clothes like they were full of coons. In fact, the pants *were* full of coons!

Two medium-sized raccoons barely escaped from inside the blue jeans, scampering away as the hounds went through my clean, dry wash piece by piece.

As to how all this happened, my husband just explained, "Well, when they get in the pants, those coons, they can cause all sorts of trouble." But in the morning, he didn't remember he'd said that.

APRIL
2018

This spring is like a groundhog
that's seen its shadow
and has gone back to winter's drawing board,
that's letting windy horses
with ragged flowing manes graze in its pasture,
that wakes up every morning with amnesia,
that's letting the first flowers dwindle
like harbor lights seen
from cloud-rigged vessels drifting out to sea,
that's like a boy with downcast eyes
holding a bouquet behind his back
waiting for his girl.

Robert Paschell

The Gregorian Calendar

S	M	T	W	T	F	S
1	2	3	4	5	6	7
8	9	10	11	12	13	14
15	16	17	18	19	20	21
22	23	24	25	26	27	28
29	30					

Litany in Middle Spring

Middle Spring invites an endless litany of events, everything connected through coincidence. Just as skunk cabbage starts to produce its foliage, the first major wave of wildflowers comes into bloom: inflorescence of bloodroot, Dutchman's britches, twinleaf, toothwort and Virginia bluebells joining the hepatica, spring beauties, lesser celandine and violet cress of March.

Plums and pears, red quinces, service berries, crab apples and cherries blossom. Redbud branches turn violet as their buds stretch and crack. Pastures and winter wheat shine with the brightest green of the year. No-till fields are violet with henbit.

Watercress blooms in quiet pools and backwaters. New tulips open. Violets and small-flowered buttercups appear in the lawn. Shoots of Japanese knotweed, hosta, phlox and lupine emerge beside the daffodils and grape hyacinths, scilla, puschkinias and windflowers still in bloom. Patches of dandelions foretell the great dandelion bloom of Middle Spring's second and third weeks

Toad trillium, early meadow rue and May apples push up out of the ground. Cowslip and ragwort bud in the swamps. Some sweet rockets and money plants are poised to send out their flower stalks. Touch-me-not sprouts have four leaves. Garden clematis tendril climb their trellises.

Bleeding hearts and poison hemlock are bushy and more than a foot tall. Rhubarb leaves are bigger than a big man's hand, and some of its fruit has succumbed to pie. Nettles and leafcup are six to eight inches tall, Asiatic lilies and columbine three to five inches, veronica and coneflower leaves an inch or two, scarlet peony stalks a foot and a half. Velvety wild ginger unfolds. September's beggarticks sprout, and the grass is long enough to cut.

Robins and cardinals call almost an hour before sunrise. Goldfinches have more than half their summer color. Small azure butterflies and white cabbage butterflies fly out for nectar. Mosquitoes, born in last month's warmth, seek gardeners in the garden.

In ponds and brooks, rushes and purple loosestrife, water lilies and pickerel plants rise from the shallows. Water striders and small diving water beetles pursue their prey. Grass snakes wait for flies and beetles in the sun. Toads cry out on milder evenings.

All of these events of litany and so many more take place both in concert and in syncopated sequence. They fashion a running narrative with interdependent threads of story, sharing as well as making this precise space and time, creating a web of beauty and utility which forms and nurtures the world.

Phases of the Golding Goldfinch Moon and the Termite Swarming Moon

As daffodils come to bloom and the dun winter feathers of goldfinches turn to gold, it is not uncommon to see swarms of ant-like creatures (termites) flying in search of new breeding and feeding grounds. When termites swarm, carpenter bees emerge to invade home siding and eaves, usually returning to the same places they were the year before, drilling and making nests, often leaving telltale piles of sawdust as signs of their activity.

April 8: The Golding Goldfinch Moon enters its final phase at 2:17 a.m. and reaches apogee the same day at 12:32 a.m.

April 15: The Swarming Termite Moon is new at 8:57 p.m.

April 20: The moon reaches perigee at 9:44 a.m.

April 22: The moon enters its second quarter at 4:45 p.m.

April 29: The moon is full at 7:58 p.m.

Meteorology

Seven major cold fronts move across the nation in an average April. Snow is possible in Northern areas with the arrival of the first three fronts. Average dates for the weather systems to reach the Mississippi: April 2, 6, 11, 16, 21, 24 and 28.

Major storms are most likely to occur on the

days between April 1 and 11, and between April 19 through the 27. Although the intensity of the high-pressure systems moderates after the 22nd, be alert for frost at least two days after each system pushes through your area.

New moon on April 15, perigee on April 20 and full moon on April 29 are expected to intensify the weather systems near those dates. In general, most precipitation usually occurs during the first two weeks of the month.

The S.A.D. Stress Index

April brings the day's length and the chances for mild weather into single digits on the S.A.D. Stress Index scale. Only the cloud column holds out at March levels, but that is not enough to keep the Index from dipping into the gentle 30s when the moon enters its second and fourth phases.

Key for Interpreting the S.A.D. Index:
Totals of 100 to 80: Severe stress
79 to 55: Severe to moderate stress
54 to 40: Moderate stress
39 to 25: Light to moderate stress
24 and below: Light stress

Day	Clouds	Weather	Daylight	Moon	Totals
April 1:	16	11	10	24	61
April 8:	14	10	9	0	33
April 15:	14	9	9	20	52
April 20:	13	8	8	22	51
April 22:	13	7	7	12	39
April 29:	12	7	7	25	51

The Sun

Cross-Quarter Day is April 21, halfway between equinox and solstice, and the Sun enters the Late Spring sign of Taurus on the same date.

The Planets

♃ ♄ ♂ ♀

Jupiter will be visible in the southwest before sunrise this month, followed by Mars and Saturn in Sagittarius along the southern horizon. Venus is the giant evening star in Aries throughout April, setting in the far west right after sundown.

The Stars

Early in the month, Orion, in its Middle Spring position, is setting in the far west after dark. Behind him high in the southwest come Gemini and Cancer. Directly overhead, the Big Dipper's pointers (that point directly to the North Star) are positioned almost exactly north-south.

The Shooting Stars

The Lyrid Meteors are active after midnight between Cygnus and Hercules during the second and third week of April, peaking on April 22 and

23. These shooting stars often appear at the rate of 15 to 25 per hour. The crescent moon should not interfere with meteor watching.

Peak Activity Times for Creatures

The following guide to lunar position shows when the moon is above (Best times) or below (Second-best times) the country, and, therefore, the periods during which livestock, people, fish and game are typically the most active and the hungriest.

Date	Best	Second-Best
April 1 – 7:	Midnight to Dawn	Afternoons
April 8 – 14:	Mornings	Evenings
April 15 – 21:	Afternoons	Midnight to Dawn
April 22 - 29:	Evenings	Mornings
April 30 – 31:	Midnight to Dawn	Afternoons

Calendar of Feast Days and Holidays for Farmers, Gardeners and Homesteaders

April 1 – June 15, 2018: Plan ahead to serve the **graduation cookout market**. College graduations can start as early as the first week in April and extend into the middle of June.

April 1, 2018: Roman Easter: Save your newly weaned, milk-fed lambs and kids, weighing about 25 to 45 pounds and not older than three months, for this market. Light-colored meat is best, a sign of the suckling animal.

April 8, 2018: Orthodox Easter: Animals for this market should also be milk fed. They can be a little bit bigger than the Roman Easter lambs or kids (between 40 and 60 pounds), though, and should be nice and fat.

April 13 – 15, 2018:   **New Year's Day** for immigrants from Cambodia, Thailand and Laos. The Asian market often favors animals in the 60 to 80-pound live-weight range.

The Almanack Daybook
for April of 2018

1: This first day past full moon is Roman (traditional) Easter and the start of the Graduation Cookout market. The Golding Goldfinch Moon wanes throughout the next two weeks, favoring the transplanting of trees, shrubs and perennials and the seeding of turnips, carrots and salsify in the Midwest, the planting of peanuts in the South, sugar beets in the North.

2: The April 2 high-pressure system initiates an eleven-day period of unsettled weather that brings an increased chance of tornadoes in the South and Midwest and spring thunderstorms to the North. This April 2 cold wave and the next are usually the last systems to threaten a light freeze in the South.

3: The field and garden day is increasing at the rate of two minutes per 24 hours. Japanese beetle grubs move to the surface of the ground to feed. Bluegills and rock bass look for worms.

4: As the moon wanes, dig in new strawberry, raspberry and blackberry plants. Dust roses as new leaves emerge. Put in early sweet corn, head lettuce and peas. Only six to seven weeks before the most tender plants can be placed outdoors.

5: All across the country, farmers plant oats and spring barley Field corn planting is underway throughout the South and the central states. Cotton planters plant cotton along the Gulf.

6: Several days before the arrival of the April 6 cold front, the chances for frost briefly diminish, and possibility of highs in the 70s or 80s increases dramatically across the country. Precipitation, however, often puts a stop to field and garden planting. After the front passes east, the possibility of damage to flowering fruit trees increases.

7: Haying begins throughout many Southern states in April; transition animals slowly from last year's old hay to this year's fresh hay.

8: Today is Orthodox Easter. Also on this date, the Golding Goldfinch Moon enters its final phase and reaches apogee, a combination which eliminates almost all S.A.D. in most people.

9: Crab apple and cherry blossom time begins in the Lower Midwest and all across the East, and it usually lasts into the last week of the month.

10: Flea season has begun for pets and livestock, and flies infest the barn.

11: After the April 11 high-pressure system crosses the country, several dry days often follow in its wake. This is the period during which to complete Middle Spring planting. Gardeners pick strawberries in Alabama and Louisiana. Along the beaches of the Northeast, piping plovers are returning to establish their nests.

12: Trees are in full flower throughout the Central Plains, the Northeast, the Northwest and the Rocky Mountains. In the Southeast, all the grasses are coming into bloom. In the Great Lakes region, commercial cabbage transplanting is underway.

13: During this fourth lunar quarter, destroy tent caterpillars as they hatch and plant all your remaining root crops. Weeds are taking over the garden; the moon's fourth phase favors removing them.

14: Throughout the country's midsection, black and gray morel mushrooms come up at this time of the month, the same time that orchard grass is ready to harvest and May apples are fully emerged. When ticks and mosquitoes become troublesome, the morel season is about over.

15: The Swarming Termite Moon is new today. The juniper webworm emerges, and Eastern tent caterpillars may begin to weave webs on flowering fruit trees. Five more weeks in the North to frost free gardening.

16: Under the power of the new moon, the days prior to the arrival of the mid-April high-pressure ridge can be expected to carry rain or snow, and are often the wettest of all April days; after this front, however, a major increase in the average daily amount of sunlight occurs: a rise from early April's 50/50 chance for sun or clouds up to a brighter 70 percent chance for clear to partly cloudy conditions.

17: In the Northwest, kestrel hawks nest and aspens flower. Wood ticks follow the receding snow, and grizzly bears come out of hibernation. In Vermont, trout fishing time begins.

18: Between now and the first of May, most dandelions go to seed along the 40th Parallel.

19: The daffodils bloom in Minneapolis. Azaleas are open in Norfolk, rhododendrons in St. Louis. Dogwoods are at their best in Atlanta. Along the north Atlantic coast, mackerel move toward inshore waters.

20: The moon reaches powerful perigee this morning, increasing the likelihood of storms and frost with the April 21 cold front.

21: After the April 21 cold front moves to the Atlantic, chances for snow decline below ten percent in almost the entire country. However, the second major tornado period of April begins now, lasting in most years until April 27.

22: The moon enters its mild second quarter this afternoon. Aphid infestations move north from the Deep South into the field and garden. Iris borers hatch; check your roots. In Vermont, spring peepers peep and loons mate.

23: Weevils emerge in alfalfa. Watercress flowers open for salads.

24: Following the April 24 cold front and weakened by proximity to the moon's entry into its second quarter, chances for frost virtually disappear in the South and become relatively insignificant throughout much of the North.

25: The high leaf canopy fills in, casting shade on the flower and vegetable garden.

26: Late Spring, a season that completes the blooming of Middle Spring's woodland flowers, arrives as admiral butterflies hatch and field grasses are long enough to ripple in the wind.

27: Average high temperatures reach 70 degrees along the Ohio River while cutworms and sod webworms work the cornfields. Baltimore Orioles begin to appear in the Midwest, and Osage trees come into bloom, along with lily-of-the-valley beneath them.

28: The first cold front of Late Spring is due near this date, enhanced by tomorrow's full moon.

29: The moon is full this evening, increasing the risk of frost along and above the 40th Parallel.

30: Highs in the 90s become possible as far north as Chicago, and the chances for a high in the 80s pass the 20 percent mark at lower elevations along the 40th Parallel.

A Note on Planting Beans

I have found that soil temperatures generally follow the normal average air temperatures within maybe ten degrees. But in the spring and early summer, the ground often lags behind the weather, causing considerable anguish to the farmer and gardener.

For example, if your beans go in before the earth is warm enough, they rot where you lay them. "Nothing sprouts," says the Greek sage, Theophrastus, "before its proper time."

On the other hand, two old-time suggestions may be useful in helping you decide when to plant.

The first, from an ancient English herbal, is popular but tricky:
"The best of growers have the seedsman go unclad to sow the field."

As long as the feet are bare, too, the technique

can be quite effective; remember, however, the soil is what you want to check, not the air.

To be on the safe side, you may wish to conduct a more reliable and potentially less controversial soil test in this clever verse by the Marquis de Croissant (1834-1897): "If the ground be warm to the derriere, 'Twill surely give thee beans to spare."

Almanack Literature
A Terrible Outhouse Afternoon
By Willy O'Holleran, Cincinnati, Ohio

Here was the situation. My wife and I had just bought this gentleman's farm in rural southern Indiana. Actually, it was not such a gentlemanly farm; in fact, it was all run down, and parts of it were falling apart.

Now there was an outhouse, a big four-holer, kind of close to the main house, and it was in need of so much repair that I decided it would have to come down.

"It's really kind of cute," my wife said, but I said that it wasn't cute enough to fix up. So one afternoon when she and her sister went shopping at the mall in Cincinnati, I decided to tear down the four holer and save some of the lumber for repairs to the chicken coop.

So I got my new crowbar and hammer, pulled open the outhouse door, walked in and fell right through the rotten floor.

On the way down, I knew I was in trouble. Deep trouble. That is because I was going down headfirst. I put out my hands to break the fall. That worked a little, and I managed to spin around just a bit so that I landed all twisted up instead of on my head, on a whole bunch of trash that people had tossed down the holes through the years.

Things could have been worse, I thought to myself. But then I realized they were getting worse by the second. My right leg and left arm were beginning to hurt, and I couldn't move my fingers on my left hand, and I was wedged in a strange kind of way so that when I tried to sit upright my leg went into all kinds of pain.

Well, there it was. How long did my wife shop? Forever. How long did it take her to find me? Even longer. How long was it before the rescue squad could lift me out? Even longer. How long did it take for my broken bones to heal? Even longer still. How long did we farm in the gentleman's fashion? Not very long.

MAY
2018

Wide are the meadows of night,
And daisies are shining there,
Tossing their lovely dews,
Lustrous and fair;
And through these sweet fields go,
Wand'rers 'mid the stars---
Venus, Mercury, Uranus, Neptune,
Saturn, Jupiter, Mars.
'Tired in their silver, they move,
And circling, whisper and say,
Fair are the blossoming meads of delight
Through which we stray.

Walter de la Mare, "Wanderers"

The Gregorian Calendar

S	M	T	W	T	F	S
		1	2	3	4	5
6	7	8	9	10	11	12
13	14	15	16	17	18	19
20	21	22	23	24	25	26
27	28	29	30	31		

The Hinge of Early Summer

On the hinge of early summer along the 40th

Parallel, the balance of time and vegetation wavers and swings each day, inventories on either side holding seasonal tides in opposition, residue in compensation with new sprouts.

This is a pivotal time that appears to be all in the favor of summer, but really it is a door that opens back to spring, as well, allowing a kind of simultaneous passage to and from, eddies in the solar tides, receding and proceeding.

On one side, the blossoms of Late Spring: the pink sweet rockets, the yellow swamp buttercups, the pale blue waterleaf, the violet wild geraniums, white Solomon's plume, deep purple larkspur and columbine, the golden-pollen clustered snakeroot, the iris, the poppies, the peonies, the catchweed with its sticky burs, the wisteria, the honeysuckles, weigelas, mock orange, the high locust clusters, yellow poplars and the fading privets.

On the other side, the side of Early Summer: parsnips, hemlock, orange day lilies, small, golden stella d'oro lilies, purple coneflowers, daisies, fruit of black raspberries and mulberries and strawberries, the lush catalpas, the blossoming elderberries and panicled dogwoods, multiflora roses, crown vetch, pink spirea, yellow and white sweet clover, Canadian thistles, nodding thistles, chicory and the paling winter wheat.

The sides of time may overlap, and a drive south two hundred miles from the 40th Parallel even opens Middle Summer; a trip two hundred miles north reveals the lost Middle Spring.

The hinge of seasons is loose and easy, swinging with the north wind and then with the south, the east and west winds. Revolving time turns with shadows and sun, splaying the variegated landscape along the tilt of the spinning Earth.

The Phases of the Termite Swarming Moon and the Daddy Longlegs Moon

Familiar to almost everyone who looks at the grass once in a while, the daddy longlegs emerges in Middle and Late Spring. The daddy longlegs announce allergy season and the filling in of the high canopy of leaves. Tadpoles swim in the shallows and strawberries ripe when daddy longlegs appear. Clovers bloom in fields and lawns, and the latest woodland flowers reach full bloom.

May 5: The Swarming Termite Moon reaches apogee at 7:35 p.m.

May 7: The moon enters its final quarter at 9:08 p.m.

May 15: The Daddy Longlegs Moon is new at 6:47 a.m.

May 17: The moon reaches perigee at 4:05 p.m.

May 22: The moon enters its second quarter at 10:49 p.m.

May 29: The moon is full at 9:19 a.m.

Meteorology

The cold fronts of Late Spring usually cross the Mississippi on or about May 2, 7, 12, 15, 21, 24 and 29.

Tornadoes, floods or prolonged periods of soggy pasture are most likely to occur within the following windows: May 3 – 12 and May 17 – 24. The last days of May and the first week of June are often soaked by the Strawberry Rains.

New moon on May 15, lunar perigee on May 17 and full moon on May 29 could contribute to unseasonable cold and to unstable meteorological conditions.

The S.A.D. Stress Index

May brings an easing of seasonal affective disorder for the majority of people in the Northern Hemisphere. The summer-like day's length, the gentle weather of spring, and the gradually decreasing cloud cover, contribute to the start of the least stressful period of the year. The S.A.D. Index reflects these changes, dipping to 19 by May 7 and registering two days in the 20s for the first time this year.

Key for Interpreting the S.A.D. Index:

Totals of 100 to 80: Severe stress
79 to 55: Severe to moderate stress
54 to 40: Moderate stress
39 to 25: Light to moderate stress
24 and below: Light stress

Day	Clouds	Weather	Daylight	Moon	Totals
May 1:	11	6	6	24	47
May 5:	10	5	6	0	21
May 7:	10	4	5	0	19
May 15:	9	5	4	20	38
May 17:	9	8	4	23	44
May 22:	8	8	3	5	24
May 29:	6	6	1	25	38

The Sun

On May 9, the Sun reaches three-fourths of the way to summer solstice. It enters the early summer sign of Gemini on May 21.

The Planets

♃ ♄ ♂ ♀

Now in Capricorn, Mars rises after midnight and moves into the southern sky before dawn. Venus is the giant evening star in Taurus setting into the far west after sundown. Jupiter, remaining in Libra, moves into the far southwest during the early morning in the first days of May; then it reappears as an evening star in the southeast by the middle of the month. Saturn in Sagittarius, rises after midnight, then disappears into the Sun as dawn approaches.

The Stars

Orion has disappeared from the night sky, a sign that Middle Spring is turning to Late Spring. Without Orion, one way to follow the warmer months of the year is to keep track of the boxy formation of Libra in the southwest, followed by the scorpion-like constellation of Scorpius. Watch them move across the southern sky all summer.

The Shooting Stars

The Eta Aquarids are active from April 18 through May 28, with the most meteors expected on May 7 and 8. The moon is not expected to interfere with meteor watching.

Peak Activity Times for Creatures

The following guide to lunar position shows when the moon is above (Best times) or below (Second-best times) the country, and, therefore, the period during which livestock, people, fish and game are typically the most active and the hungriest.

Date	Best	Second-Best
May 1 – 6:	Midnight to Dawn	Afternoons
May 7 – 14 :	Mornings	Evenings
May 15 – 21:	Afternoons	Midnight to Daw
May 22 – 29:	Evenings	Mornings
May 30 – 31:	Midnight to Dawn	Afternoons

Calendar of Feast Days and Holidays for Farmers, Gardeners and Homesteaders

May 13, 2018: Mother's Day

May 15, 2018: Ramadan begins at sunset. Now is

the time to advertise your farm to the Halal market in preparation for the close of Ramadan on June 14.

May 28, 2018: Memorial Day

The Almanack Daybook
for May of 2018

1: The first cool front of May coincides with the darkening moon, and it is a good marker for spring worming, weaning lambs and kids, clipping feet and dipping for external parasites. In the fields, fight armyworms and corn borers. Attack carpenter bees around the barn. The dark moon also favors traditional worm control methods such as liming the pasture, planting garlic and plowing in mustard.

2: In the Northeast and Upper Midwest, it is time for tulips, azaleas and rhododendrons.

3: As conditions permit, sow seeds for forages that will provide as close to year-round grazing as possible: tall fescue, ryegrass, wheat, oats and rape for Early Spring; Kentucky bluegrass and orchard grass for spring and fall; bromegrass and timothy for early summer; birdsfoot trefoil, bahiagrass, Bermuda grass, Sudan grass, crabgrass and lespedeza for mid to late summer.

4: Silver olive bushes come into bloom, just when sweet gum, mountain maples and white mulberry trees flower. In the woods, wild strawberries and bellwort have golden blossoms. Poppies and daisies open in the garden.

5: Lunar apogee today should soften the high-pressure system due around May 7 and lessen the chance for frost to the northern half of the country.

6: Lunar conditions are favorable for planting the rest of your root crops, transplanting shrubs and trees and working with all your animals.

7: The moon enters its gentle final quarter this evening. In the woods, golden seal and Solomon's seal are blooming. Rhododendrons fill with color, and locusts, black walnut trees and oaks come into flower all along the 40th Parallel.

8: The cutting of hay moves north toward the Canadian border at the rate of about one hundred miles a week, and it will be taking place almost everywhere by the middle of June.

9: Animals given dry hay before being let out to new pastures tend to gorge themselves less and develop bloat far less frequently.

10: Spring rains and humidity can increase the risk of internal parasites in livestock. Consider using stool sample analysis to ensure that drenching has been effective.

11: When mock orange, sweet Cicely, Robin's fleabane, chives, catmint, waterleaf, wild raspberry, shooting star, peonies, sweet rockets and May apples come into bloom, conditions may be just right to move all your livestock to pasture.

12: The cold front that arrives around this date is one of the last frost-bearing fronts to move across the nation. Although gardens in the North are not immune to a freeze throughout the entire month of May, the greatest danger of loss from low temperatures recedes quickly as this high moves out over the Atlantic.

13: When the first day lily opens, you should have all your corn in the ground, and it should have sprouted, too. If you don't have day lilies, the first thistles bloom around the same time.

14: Spring wheat has often been planted in the North by now, and all the oats should be in the ground between Denver and New York. Potatoes, commercial tomatoes and pickles have all been set out by the end of the month along the Great Lakes. Winter wheat is at least a foot high across the central states and will soon be pale golden green below the Mason-Dixon Line.

15: The Daddy Longlegs Moon is new this morning, strengthening the May 15 cold front and increasing the chances for light frost down into the Ohio Valley. This front and the next two high-pressure systems are often followed by the Strawberry Rains, the wettest time of May in the Lower Midwest, the Mid Atlantic states and the East.

16: Flea beetles, damselflies and leafhoppers become active and field crickets sing as snapping turtles lay their eggs.

17: The danger of frost continues as the moon reaches perigee this afternoon, strengthening the meteorological and psychological effects of new moon and the cool front of May 15.

18: Clover season spreads throughout the country this month. Relatives of alfalfa, the small black medic, purple vetch and the weedy yellow and white sweet clover surge along the roadsides as well as in pastures.

19: In the Northern forests, pines, spruce, hemlock, arbor vitae, alders and birch reach the height of their bloom.

20: All along the 40th Parallel, the canopy of leaves closes within the next week or two, with maples and box elders coming in during late spring, sycamores and oaks at the beginning of summer.

21: Lunar conditions finally favor low stress in humans and other beasts.

22: The moon enters its gentle second quarter this afternoon.

23: After locust trees are done flowering, then snow-on-the-mountain blossoms and sweet

Williams, clematis and spiderwort open. White-spotted skippers and red admiral butterflies visit the garden.

24: The May 24 high-pressure system is usually the last frost-bearing front to Northern gardens.

25: The third and final major wave of songbird migration reaches the Great Lakes in the last days of May, dominated by female magnolia, Canada and bay-breasted warblers, the American redstart, indigo buntings, the vireos and flycatchers. By the middle of June, virtually all migrations are complete, and nesting has begun in the marshes.

26: Throughout the country's midsection, cottonwood cotton is in the wind, signaling the start of elderberry and chicory blooming season. Honewort blossoms in the woods, cow parsnip in the wetlands.

27: Unstable meteorological conditions are likely to precede the last cold front of May, especially since the moon will be full near its arrival.

28: Gather pie cherries, mulberries and black raspberries. The fat moon should make them extra juicy.

29: Rain is often heavy as the final front of May approaches, and today's full moon increases the likelihood of storms. When this high moves away, however, it usually leaves sunny, dry conditions.

30: Fertilize asparagus and rhubarb as their seasons end. Side dress the corn.

31: Pollen from grasses reaches its peak in the central portions of the United States, as bluegrass, orchard grass, timothy, red top and Bermuda grass all continue to flower.

Almanack Literature
Blue Racers Can Kill1
By Anna Monroe Bruce, Fairborn, Ohio

When my mom was a young girl, she and her girl friend in Kentucky were going to Sunday school over the mountain and through the woods, talking to each other as they hurried along.

All at once, her friend screamed again and again, falling to the ground crying: "Get help! Get help!" Momma ran to the foot of the mountain to the church house where several men were standing. They came to meet Momma. She told them what had happened. One man jerked his knife out of his pocket and they all ran to the girl.

They found her lying unconscious on the ground, her clothes drawn very tightly around her waist. The man took his knife and cut what looked like a cord that was tight around her. That cord turned out to be a snake, and it fell into four pieces on the ground.

The creature was called a blue racer. They are not poisonous, and they do not bite their prey, but this one had had almost squeezed the girl to death by circling her body and drawing tighter and tighter.

They revived Momma's friend with resuscitation and she lived. But she and my mother did not walk over the mountain and woods to Sunday school any more. They went the long way by the road from then on.

JUNE
2018

The exuberance of June…It began at daybreak with the chirping and chattering of birds close at hand and in widening circles around us. And then, what greater wonder than the rising of the sun? Even the nights, as yet without insect choirs, were alive. Fireflies against the mass of trees were flashing galaxies which repeatedly made and unmade abstract patterns of light, voiceless as the stars overhead….

Harlan Hubbard

The Gregorian Calendar

S	M	T	W	T	F	S
					1	2
3	4	5	6	7	8	9
10	11	12	13	14	15	16
17	18	19	20	21	22	23
24	25	26	27	28	29	30

Spiders

I have always been partial toward spiders. My mother, a stay-at-home mom who spent a lot of time in the basement washing clothes (refusing to use an automatic washer), always talked fondly of them. I recall that she named two of her eight-legged companions Hopeful and Shy. They were her friends, she told me. Why that was so, she didn't say.

As a child, I just accepted the idea that spiders were good. I dismissed the idea of spiders biting and poisoning a person as pretty unlikely, considering those creatures were my mother's allies.

So I have lived my life in harmony with spiders, protecting them when I can, only intervening in their activities occasionally to save a moth or butterfly. And I usually encounter my favorite spiders, the micrathenas and the orb weavers, at the end of late summer and the beginning of autumn.

The micrathenas are small, odd-shaped arachnids that build their webs across my hiking paths, especially in the woods. Although they start their activities in middle summer, it is toward the end of August that they are most common.

Two kinds of orb weavers work in my yard, a long-bodied variety that places its web above my small pond starting in July, and a larger, round-bodied variety that always seems to create its traps across the door to my tool shed in September and October.

Like wooly-bear caterpillars, these spiders are prophets of cold to come. As well, they are models of industry and foresight. They do not hide their activities in basements, but they do seem hopeful and shy. Most important: they spin a connection between my mother and me in this thin time of autumn, reminding me of friendships past and still to be.

The Daddy Longlegs Moon and the Turtle Hatching Moon

While daddy longlegs seek food and mates in spring, many varieties of turtles lay their eggs near rivers and lakes. You can know when the turtles are hatching and the daddy longlegs nurturing their eggs when hemlock and parsnips bloom by the side of the road, when poison ivy flowers, when chiggers bite and wild black raspberries ripen.

June 2: The Daddy Longlegs Moon reaches apogee at 11:34 a.m.

June 6: The moon enters its final quarter at 1:31 p.m.

June 13: The Turtle Hatching Moon is new at 2:43 p.m.

June 14: The moon reaches perigee at 6:55 p.m.

June 20: The moon enters its second quarter at 5:51 a.m.

June 27: The moon is full at 11:53 p.m.

June 29: The moon reaches apogee at 9:43 p.m.

Meteorology

The cool fronts associated with Early Summer typically cross the Mississippi on or about June 2, 6, 10, 15, 23 and 29. Major storms are most likely to occur on the days between June 5 - 8, June 13 - 16 and June 24 - 28.

New moon on June 13 (followed by perigee on the 14th) increases the chances for freezing temperatures along the Canadian border and at higher elevations. Full moon on June 27 could contribute to unstable meteorological conditions in conjunction with the June 29 cool front.

The S.A.D. Stress Index

Unless the weather is unseasonably hot, few people suffer from S.A.D. in June. The Index reveals a rare window in the year during which astronomical and meteorological factors that cause stress are reduced to almost nothing.

Key for Interpreting the S.A.D. Index:
Totals of 100 to 80: Severe stress
79 to 55: Severe to moderate stress
54 to 40: Moderate stress
39 to 25: Light to moderate stress
24 and below: Light stress

Day	Clouds	Weather	Daylight	Moon	Total
June 1:	4	4	0	10	18
June 6:	3	2	0	0	5
June 14:	2	2	0	25	29
June 20:	0	0	0	0	0
June 27:	0	2	0	20	22
June 28:	3	5	0	10	19

The Sun

Summer solstice occurs on June 21 at 5:07 a.m., the Sun entering the middle summer sign of Cancer at the same time. Between June 19 and 23, the Sun holds steady at its solstice declination of 23 degrees 26 minutes, and the day's length remains virtually unchanged.

The Planets

Mars, remaining in Capricorn, moves along the

southern horizon between midnight and dawn. Venus in Cancer is the giant western evening star. Continuing to accompany Libra, Jupiter shines in the southern sky at dusk. Saturn in Sagittarius is visible in the early morning sky until the end of the month.

The Stars

Continuing to follow the year in stars, find Early Summer's boxy (or teapot shaped) Libra due south, with Scorpius close behind. If you look up to the middle of the sky, you will see a horseshoe-shaped constellation, the Corona Borealis, and to its right the bright planting star, Arcturus.

Peak Activity Times for Creatures

The following guide to lunar position shows when the moon is above (Best times) or below (Second-best times) the country, and, therefore, the period during which livestock, people, fish and game are typically the most active and the hungriest.

Date	Best	Second-Best
June 1 – 5:	Midnight to Dawn	Afternoons
June 6 – 12 :	Mornings	Evenings
June 13 – 19:	Afternoons	Midnight to Dawn
June 20 – 26:	Evenings	Mornings
June 27 – 30:	Midnight to Dawn	Afternoons

Calendar of Feast Days and Holidays for Farmers, Gardeners and Homesteaders

June 14, 2018: Id al Fitr: The Festival of the breaking of the Ramadan Fast: Sheep for this market should not be older than a year. Castrated or uncastrated males are acceptable, as are ewes. The best weight for Ramadan sheep is around 60 pounds, but weaned lambs between 45 and 115 pounds are often used. In reviewing your culling program, consider that older sheep often command higher prices during this period.

June 17, 2018: Father's Day

The Almanack Daybook
for June of 2018

1: June is the month (April and May in the South) during which insect infestations typically reach the economic threshold.

2: The Daddy Longlegs Moon is at apogee today. A cool front crosses the nation near this date; it may bring a light freeze at higher elevations, but apogee should weaken the strength of that weather system elsewhere. Throughout the East and lower Midwest, the Rugosa rose, floribunda rose, delphinium, moth mullein, feverfew, heliopsis, quickweed, swamp valerian, moneywort and rape come into bloom.

3: June is haying month in the upper half of the nation. Legumes should give your animals better nutrition and weight if you cut fields right after they bloom.

4: The canopy has closed above the woodland wildflowers when winter wheat is a soft pale green and the clovers and vetches are all blooming in the fields.

5: The moon enters its final quarter tomorrow. The darkening moon is right for all kinds of animal care (especially worming and spraying for external parasites), for planting root crops, shrubs and trees, and for weeding and mulching, as well as insect hunting.

6: The low-pressure system that accompanies the June 6 front initiates a four-day period during which there is an increased chance for tornadoes and flash floods.

7: Canadian thistles and crown vetch open in the fields and pastures. Oakleaf hydrangeas blossom in the city, pickerel plants in ponds, balloon flowers in gardens.

8: Harvest canola, commercial broccoli and squash. Begin the winter wheat harvest in the South. Consider putting in double-crop soybeans after the wheat is cut.

9: Yucca plants flower, and young grackles have left their nests. Plant the vegetable garden for

August and September harvests.

10: The sunniest June days usually occur between now and the 26th, and the first major heat wave often develops across the Gulf states and the central states.

11: Throughout the country's midsection, harvest beans and squash, strawberries, pie cherries and the first black raspberries.

12: New moon time is favorable for pruning shrubs and trees that flowered earlier in the year.

13: The Turtle Hatching Moon is new today. Plan to put in the last of the hot-weather vegetables (like tomatoes, squash, eggplant and peppers).

14: The moon reaches perigee, its position closest to Earth. Combined with the new moon, perigee increases the possibility for chilly weather and mid-June precipitation.

15: Adding to the effects of new moon and perigee, a cool front is expected to cross the Mississippi between June 13 and 16, and it is likely to be a stormy weather system.

16: The waxing moon favors the continuing harvest of strawberries and spring vegetables.

17: In the gardens of town and country throughout the East and Midwest, lily season creates a crescendo of color that peaks in four to five weeks.

18: Pokeweed, thimble plant, wood mint, figwort, tall nettle and black-eyed Susans flower in the fields. Avens and enchanter's nightshade open in the woods, lizard's tail in the rivers and lakes.

19: Thistles go to seed as corn borers eat the corn and early soybeans bloom.

20: The moon enters its weak second quarter today, favorable for vacations and outings of all kinds (because it minimizes lunar stress).

21: Rose of Sharon bushes produce pink, white and violet blossoms throughout the South.

22: Strawberry season ends while domestic red raspberries and wild black raspberries ripen.

23: The June 23 high-pressure system is typically cool and dry, and it is often followed by some of the sunniest and driest days of all the year.

24: The wheat harvest begins in the Lower Midwest, bright orange butterfly weed reaches full bloom and acorns (a favorite food of deer) become fully formed.

25: Middle Summer typically begins near this date and lasts through the middle of August's second week. In those six to seven weeks, approximately an hour is lost from the day's length along the 40th Parallel, and the year turns toward autumn.

26: After summer solstice, the percentage of totally sunny days is the highest of the year throughout the nation.

27: Apogee weakens the power of today's full moon, decreasing chances for storms.

28: The final weather system of the month is often followed by the Corn Tassel Rains, a two-week period of intermittent precipitation that accompanies the Dog Days of middle summer.

29: This waning moon is especially favorable for detasseling corn, for harvesting winter wheat, for completing the first cut of alfalfa and for beginning the second cut.

30: In spite of the association of the Corn Tassel Rains with heat, the final two days of June are sometimes the coldest of the year's midsection, highs below 80 degrees occurring more than half the time above the Border States.

Almanack Literature
Surprise in the Outhouse
By Aldon Cisco, Waverly, Ohio

This story starts in Frankfort, Ohio on a piece of property my father-in-law, Bankie E., bought for a getaway. This property had an old building on it that resembled an old corncrib. We remodeled it and equipped it with linoleum, insulation, electricity, radio, card table, air conditioning, stove, refrigerator and bunk beds.

And we needed an outhouse, so we built one, a one-holer. My father-in-law, Bankie, dug a hole and took a 55-gallon drum and knocked three or four holes in the bottom and put it in the hole, and then we set the outhouse on the barrel, kind of open on the back side.

After a few years, the trips to the outhouse started to accumulate. My father-in-law's best friend, Velver C., who was close to 70 years old at the time, made a trip to the outhouse as nature called. Later my brother-in-law, Ronnie M. , made a trip also and came back in laughing, and we all went to see what was going on.

It seems that an opossum had gotten into the barrel and could not get out. He had mud on his head and was standing on the top of the pile with front feet outreached within six inches of the top of the seat.

This started the laughter, and to this day it is still funny to think of what could have happened. There were no lives lost or even a bite.

My father-in-law put a 2 x 4 in the barrel from the back and the opossum escaped. I would think he was one happy opossum to get out, and he must have learned his lesson because he never returned. We also learned our lesson: take a flashlight and always check the hole.

My father-in-law and his best friend are now gone, but not in our hearts and minds. The memories live on.

JULY
2018

What more felicitie can fall to creature
Than to enjoy delight with libertie,
And to be Lord of all the works of Nature,
To raigne in the aire from th'earth to highest sky,
To feed on flowers and weeds of glorious feature,
To take whatever thing does please the eie?

Edmond Spenser

The Gregorian Calendar

S	M	T	W	T	F	S
1	2	3	4	5	6	7
8	9	10	11	12	13	14
15	16	17	18	19	20	21
22	23	24	25	26	27	28
29	30	31				

Counting Lilies

It is lily blooming season, and I am counting lily blossoms in my yard. I accept that my practice has almost no socially redeeming value. I accept the fact that no one else cares (nor should they care) about the number of lily blossoms in my yard, and that the actual number does not inerest me so much as the counting itself.

I record the results of counting in my daybook, but the record does not support theories of climate change. In fact, it supports nothing at all. I am not invested in lilies, and although I like lilies, I am not trying to grow more or more beautiful lilies.

So why do I do it, really?

First, when I am counting lilies, I am not thinking of other things. For a few minutes each July day, counting lilies disconnects me from national and world problems. I do not worry about the future nor do I ruminate about the past. I just count.

Second, counting lilies is a form of procrastination. The more lilies there are, the longer I can delay doing other things that other people might find acceptable, or things that I actually should do or need to do.

Third, summer, like everything else, is a matter of accumulation. More is more. The more I see, the more I get. The more I count, the more I have.

Fourth, counting my own lilies is an utterly free practice. I compete with no one. No one else counts my lilies. No one else's lilies count. And no one sees me counting lilies or knows I count lilies (except you). Safe in the meaninglessness of counting lilies, I am loose in the world, unfettered by what is good or bad.

Fifth, I watch myself counting lilies. The more I count lilies, and the longer I count, the more years I count, the more I learn about myself. Little by little old self-definitions become diluted. What other people may or may not think of me does not matter. I am no longer this person or that person. I am neither successful nor a failure. I am neither socially responsible nor socially irresponsible, neither educated nor uneducated, strong nor weak, loved nor unloved, old nor young, respected nor unrespected. I am just a person on whatever day in July it happens to be, for a few moments, counting lilies.

The Turtle Hatching Moon and the Black-Eyed Susan Moon

July offers more wildflower seasons than any other month of the year. Led on by the ubiquitous black-eyed Susans, the purple loosestrife, Queen Anne's lace, purple coneflower, wild petunia, bouncing Bet, blue dayflower, white vervain, sow thistle, pokeweed, St. John's wort, teasel and wild lettuce (among so many others) dominate the fields. In the shade of the canopy, July is the time of wood mint, wood nettle, leafcup, touch-me-not, lopseed and avens.

July 6: The Turtle Hatching Moon enters its final quarter at 2:50 a.m.

July 12: The Black-Eyed Susan Moon is new at 9:48 p.m.

July 13: The moon reaches perigee at 3:28 a.m.

July 18: The moon enters its second phase at 2:52 p.m.

July 27: The moon is full at 3:20 p.m. and reaches apogee at 2:44 a.m.

A total eclipse of the moon occurs on July 27, but it will not be visible from most of North America.

Meteorology

The cool fronts of Middle Summer normally cross the Mississippi River around July 6, 14, 21and 28. Tornadoes, hurricanes, floods or prolonged periods of soggy pasture are most likely to occur within the weather windows of July 3 through 7, July 18 through 23.

New moon on July 12 (followed by perigee on July 13) and full moon on July 27 may increase the chance of tornadoes in the South and Midwest and the landing of a hurricane in the Gulf region near those dates.

The period between July 24 and August 5, on the other hand, is usually one of the most uneventful (except for Dog Day heat) in the entire meteorological year.

The S.A.D. Stress Index

Seasonal affective disorder increases during the hottest days of the year. Many people who suffer from humidity and high temperatures tend to stay indoors like they do in the winter; consequently, they often experience some of the same S.A.D. symptoms they feel in December or January.

Key for Interpreting the S.A.D. Index:
Totals of 100 to 80: Severe stress
79 to 55: Severe to moderate stress
54 to 40: Moderate stress
39 to 25: Light to moderate stress
24 and below: Light stress

Day	Clouds	Weather	Daylight	Moon	Total
July 1:	5	7	0	8	20
July 6:	5	10	1	0	16
July 13:	4	13	2	25	44
July 18:	2	17	3	0	22
July 27:	1	20	4	25	50

The Sun

At 10:36 a.m. on July 6, the Earth reaches aphelion, the point at which it is about 153 million kilometers (its greatest distance) from the Sun. Aphelion occurs almost exactly six months from perihelion, Earth's position closest to the Sun (about

148 million kilometers).

A partial eclipse of the Sun will occur on July 13, but it will only be visible in the southern regions of the Southern Hemisphere. The Sun enters the late summer sign of Leo on July 23.

The Planets

♃ ♄ ♀ ♂

Traveling across the southern horizon in Capricorn, Mars disappears from the morning sky by the end of July. Venus in Leo is the giant evening star in the far west after sundown. Jupiter in Libra lies along the southern horizon after dark. Saturn arrives in the evening sky with Sagittarius in the southeast.

The Stars

The boxy teapot-like star formation of Libra is prominent in the southwest, followed by Scorpius and its red center, Antares. Sagittarius, the Archer, follows the Scorpion in the southeast. Above the Archer, the Milky Way sweeps up toward Cassiopeia in the north.

At noon, the stars overhead are the stars of winter's midnight: Orion due south, the Pleiades overhead. On the clearest July afternoons, January's Sirius (the Dog Star of Middle Summer) is visible in the southeast.

The Shooting Stars

The nights of July 28 – 29 bring the Delta Aquarids after 12:00 a.m. in Aquarius. This shower can bring up to 20 meteors in an hour. The bright Moon at the end of July, however, may make meteor watching less rewarding.

Peak Activity Times for Creatures

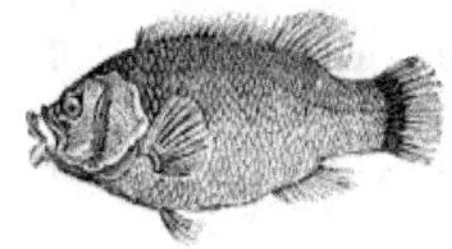

The following guide to lunar position shows when the moon is above (Best times) or below (Second-best times) the country, and, therefore, the period during which livestock, people, fish and game are typically the most active and the hungriest.

Date	Best	Second-Best
July 1 – 5:	Midnight to Dawn	Afternoons
July 6 – 11:	Mornings	Evenings
July 12 – 17:	Afternoons	Midnight to Dawn
July 18 – 26:	Evenings	Mornings
July 27 – 31:	Midnight to Dawn	Afternoons

Calendar of Feast Days and Holidays for Farmers, Gardeners and Homesteaders

July 4, 2018: United States (also Puerto Rico) Independence Day:. Offer kids and lambs for Independence Day cookouts or tailgate parties at parades and celebrations (take orders).

The Almanack Daybook
for July of 2018

1: Plan to harvest before the Corn Tassel Rains (July 2 through 7). Mulch in preparation of Dog Day heat and peak weed season.

2: In the garden, plant hollyhock, sweet William and forget-me-not seeds for next year's blossoms. When the first black walnuts start to fall, renovate strawberry beds, cutting off tops above the crown, then fertilize.

3: The best part of black raspberry season ends as the summer apple harvest gets underway. Standing water from Corn Tassel Rains can encourage parasite infestation in pastures. Roadside grasses brown in the Sun like the winter wheat.

4: The Dog Days of summer reach full bloom, and

average temperatures remain at their peak almost everywhere in the United States until July 28.

5: The cool front that typically crosses the nation in July's first week should be warmed by diminishing influence of the moon. Consequently, the sky may clear somewhat and real summer heat will begin.

6: The Turtle Hatching Moon enters its final quarter slightly lowering seasonal stress that is caused by heat-related cabin fever. This waning moon favors the harvest of grains.

7: Milkweed pods have emerged almost everywhere; they will burst at the approach of Middle Fall in three months.

8: As the July Dog Days intensify, they bring more Japanese beetles to the roses, leafhoppers to the potatoes and aphids everywhere.

9: Heat stress intensifies for summer crops. Keep flowers and vegetables well watered and fed to help them resist the onslaught of the insects and weather.

10: Morning birdsong continues to diminish, making way for the increase of insect volume. Blackberries are August size this week, but still green in the North.

11: Sycamore trees shed their bark, marking the center of summer. Set out autumn collards, kale, cabbage and broccoli in the week ahead while the moon waxes.

12: The Black-Eyed Susan Moon is new, increasing the likelihood of thunderstorms. Watch for brown spots in the lawn, signs of the sod webworm. Give plenty of water to the infected area, and treat with pyrethrums.

13: The moon reaches perigee, enhancing the power of the new moon and strengthening the mid-July weather system due around July 14. Thunderstorms could lodge the wheat still standing in the fields, and hail could shred the corn. Lunar conditions may contribute to a hurricane in the Caribbean.

14: A slight turning of the leaves begins on some of the redbuds, Virginia creepers, box elders and buckeyes. Foliage of Japanese honeysuckle and the multiflora roses often show patches of yellow.

15: Calculate estimated losses in productivity due to late planting, drought, insect infestations, hail and other problems.

16: Include the mums in your summer care; give them extra food now for extra blossoms in late August and September.

17: Midwestern peaches come to the markets as late summer's white snakeroot buds in the woods and Joe Pye weed heads up in the wetlands.

18: The moon enters its mild second phase today.

Cicadas chant full force now. The first katydids begin singing after dark, and crickets intensify their mating songs. Woolly bear caterpillars become more common. Fireflies become less numerous if the month has been dry. Fawns are third grown, but still may have their spots.

19: Dig potatoes and dry onions, cut cabbage for kraut, pickle the cucumbers, gather sweet corn, top tobacco, bring in oats, wheat, alfalfa and all the summer market crops.

20: Elderberries turn purple as soybeans blossom. Some elm and black walnut leaves yellow in the heat. Pokeweed flowers turn to berries. Seed pods form on the trumpet creepers and the locusts. Catalpa beans are full and long.

21: The July 21 cool front crosses the country, weakening Middle Summer just a little with a thunderstorm.

22: Late July, when the day's length has lost an average of 30 to 45 minutes from its longest span, is the average time for does and ewes to show first signs of estrus cycling in much of the country. Humans may feel hormonal changes at this time, as well.

23: Autumn turnip planting are often begun today, guided by the first purple blossoms of tall ironweed. Farmers prepare soil for autumn wheat planting.

24: The waxing moon, just three days from full, is likely to strengthen the July 24 high-pressure system and bring slightly cooler nights.

25: The best of the morning bird chorus is over now for the year. Swallows are migrating; they can often be seen congregating on the high wires. Shiny spicebush, boxwood, greenbrier and poison ivy berries have formed.

26: Summer apple and blueberry seasons wind down across the East. The wheat harvest ends as wild grapes ripen. Geese become restless, their goslings grown. Late-summer fogs appear at dawn.

27: The moon is full today, but it also reaches apogee, and that moon's position farthest from Earth usually weakens lunar power.

28: At the very end of July, when the Summer Triangle of stars moves overhead just before bedtime, normal average temperatures start to fall in almost every state of the Union. That means that light frost season is only three to four weeks away along the Canadian border, six to seven weeks away in the lower Midwest, and eight to ten weeks away in the northern parts of the South.

29: Some full-size Osage fruits and walnuts are heavy enough to fall to the ground in summer storms, another marker for the advance of the year.

30: Lizard's tail and wood nettle go to seed along

the riverbanks. Blackberries ripen. A few black walnut leaves are falling. Meadowlarks begin migration.

31: Farmers prepare for August seeding of alfalfa, smooth brome grass, orchard grass, tall fescue, red clover and timothy.

Almanack Literature
A Rat in the Outhouse
By the Bylers, Greenwich, Ohio

Early one morning, my uncle grabbed a paper and went to the outhouse. Sitting there reading while doing his business, he heard a rattling and a scratching. But he didn't pay much attention to it… until all at once…

He looked around and there he saw a big, fat rat coming his way, and up over his naked legs it went, and up my uncle jumped screaming and making funny noises and out the door he went.

We don't know if he was finished or not. And did he take his pants along? We don't know. But after that, he always knocked around before he went in the outhouse!

AUGUST
2018

*The backyard
overgrown with wild grape,
hollyhock, creeping charlie,
is home to a thousand
white butterflies this August....*

Ann Filemyr

The Gregorian Calendar

S	M	T	W	T	F	S
			1	2	3	4
5	6	7	8	9	10	11
12	13	14	15	16	17	18
19	20	21	22	23	24	25
26	27	28	29	30	31	

A Zillion Days

In matters of global economics, the concepts of millions and billions and trillions seem disconnected from day-to-day budgeting. Who knows, I wonder, what all those zeros at the end of whole numbers really mean?

As I watch the season progress, I realize that my sense of numbers in the world around me is equally as confused. In the middle of May, the hundred days of summer feel like a zillion days to me. My body senses a limitless promise in that span of time.

When I have just emerged from winter, I refuse to imagine the return of cold and snow. The magnitude of the new warmth and the benevolence of green leaves skew my sense of time, and I instinctively multiply the 100 days of summer by 1,000 or by 10,000, and I simply dismiss the idea all those days could ever be used up.

Then, in just a few days, maybe 50 days or so, halfway through the summer, the mathematics of self-deception fails me. Only half the days of the season are gone, but the veil of June magic has gone too. The possibility that frost could arrive in six or seven weeks suddenly makes sense. Winter suddenly makes sense, too.

Somewhere in middle summer, around the time cicadas start to sing, the illusion of an indeterminate 100 days unravels. At some point between the number 99 and the number 50, innocence is lost, self-deception revealed, and counting becomes an exercise in measuring the fragility of summer.

The Black-Eyed Susan Moon and the Blackberry Jam Moon

When flocks of ducks and geese have settled into their post-birthing routines and Middle Summer's wildflowers start to pale, then blackberries redden and then turn sweet and black, perfect for cobblers and jam. Blackberries ripen when peaches are ripe, when katydids chant through the nights and when ragweed pollen joins the thistledown drifting through the hottest days of the year.

August 4: The Black-Eyed Susan Moon enters its last quarter at 1:18 p.m.

August 10: The moon reaches perigee at 1:05 p.m.

August 11: The Blackberry Jam Moon is new at 4:57 a.m.

August 18: The moon enters its first quarter at 2:48 a.m.

August 23: The moon reaches apogee at 6:23 a.m.

August 26: The moon is full at 6:56 a.m.

Meteorology

The cool fronts of Late Summer ordinarily reach the Mississippi River around August 4, 10, 17, 21 and 29.Tornadoes, hurricanes, floods or prolonged periods of soggy pasture are most likely to occur within the weather windows of August 8 and 13 and between August 27 and 31.

Lunar perigee on August 10, new moon on August 11 and full moon on August 26 are likely to strengthen fronts due near those dates.

The S.A.D. Stress Index

In Late Summer, seasonal affective disorder typically depends more on heat and humidity than on the day's length or cloud cover.

Key for Interpreting the S.A.D. Index:
Totals of 100 to 80: Severe stress
79 to 55: Severe to moderate stress
54 to 40: Moderate stress
39 to 25: Light to moderate stress
24 and below: Light stress

Day	Clouds	Weather	Daylight	Moon	Total
August 1:	0	20	4	10	34
August 4:	0	10	4	5	19
August 10:	0	5	5	25	35
August 18:	0	15	6	0	21
August 23:	0	15	7	15	37
August 26:	0	11	9	25	45

The Sun

This month, the Sun moves halfway between summer solstice and autumn equinox, entering Virgo and reaching Cross-Quarter Day on August 23. A partial eclipse of the Sun occurs on August 11, visible in northern North America beginning at 4:47 a.m.

The Planets

All four major planets are visible after dark this month. Find Mars in Capricorn following Saturn in Sagittarius along the southeastern horizon after sundown. Venus in Virgo is the brightest evening star due west after sunset, followed by Jupiter in Libra in the southwest.

The Stars

Now Libra has moved deep into the west by 11:00 p.m., with Scorpio following close behind along the horizon. The Northern Cross (or Cygnus, the Swan) has moved directly overhead and will tell the time of year throughout the autumn until Orion appears in the east once again.

The Shooting Stars

The Perseid meteors peak August 11 through 13 in the east an hour or so after midnight below the Milky Way in Perseus. This shower can produce up to 60 meteors in an hour and will not be obscured by the moon.

Peak Activity Times for Creatures

The following guide to lunar position shows when the moon is above (Best times) or below (Second-best times) the country, and, therefore, the period during which livestock, people, fish and game are typically the most active and the hungriest.

Date	Best	Second-Best
August 1 – 3:	Midnight to Dawn	Afternoons
August 4 – 10:	Mornings	Evenings
August 11 – 17:	Afternoons	Midnight to Dawn
August 18 – 25:	Evenings	Mornings
August 26 – 31:	Midnight to Dawn	Afternoons

Calendar of Feast Days and Holidays for Farmers, Gardeners and Homesteaders

August 6, 2018: Jamaican Independence Day: Demand may increase for older lambs, rams or ewes, up to 65 pounds at this time.

August 10, 2018: Ecuadorian Independence Day: Explore marketing lambs and kids for cookouts during this celebration.

August 21 – 25: Eid Al-Adha: (Festival of Sacrifice) Lambs and kids in the range of 55 to 80 pounds are favored for this market.

The Almanack Daybook
for August of 2018

1: Average temperatures drop approximately one to two degrees a week in August, two to three degrees a week in September.

2: Ragweed pollen fills the afternoons. Golden and purple coneflowers and white, pink and violet phlox still dominate the gardens. Red trumpet vine still curls through the trellises. The pure white virgin's bower opens. Mums and red stonecrop appear in the dooryards. Prickly mallow, field thistle, clearweed, willow herb and Japanese knotweed blossom in the woods and alleys. Summer apples are half picked.

3: Even though the night grows longer in August, the percentage of possible sunshine per day increases to the highest of the year throughout the country.

4: The Black-Eyed Susan Moon enters its last quarter, and this weak lunar position should diminish the effects of the August 4 cool front. From this point on, the likelihood for highs in the 90s begins a steady decline across the northern tier of states, and the possibility for a high only in the 60s grows stronger.

5: Robin calls increase throughout the day, short clucking signals for migration. Flocks of starlings (called murmurations) spin and dive above the fields.

6: Green acorns fall from their branches. Black walnut foliage thins. Fruit of the bittersweet ripens. Spicebush berries redden.

7: Hummingbirds, wood ducks, plovers, Baltimore Orioles and purple martins start to disappear south.

8: Get ready to seed or re-seed spring pastures and green manure areas in September or October under the waxing moon.

9: Everbearing strawberries and watermelons are ripe, Midwestern peaches are at their best. Farmers are bringing in corn for silage, digging potatoes, picking tomatoes and finishing the second or third cut of alfalfa hay.

10: The August 10 cool front is often the strongest weather system of Middle and Late Summer. This year, today's lunar perigee and tomorrow's new moon are likely to greatly enhance its power and increase the chances for hurricanes in the Caribbean.

11: The Blackberry Jam Moon is new this morning. As the moon waxes during the week ahead, make blackberry jam. Plant fall peas. Put out kale and collard sets for November. Seed the lawn.

12: Gather up the winter squash plants as their stems dry, leaving about two inches of stem on the fruit; store in a cool, dry location. Make juice and wine and jelly from elderberries and wild grapes.

13: Nurseries set out their mums, and pansy time is here for the autumn pansy market.

14: Morning fogs thicken and become more frequent as the night air cools more often into the 50s and below.

15: Grackle flocking increases while cardinal song becomes fainter.

16: Today is Cross-Quarter Day, the halfway point to equinox, and an important marker for harvest and breeding preparations for sheep and goats.

17: The cool front that typically arrives near this date reinforces the transition from summer stability to autumn unpredictability.

18: The moon enters its mild second quarter. Wild plums are ready for jelly. Before frost, pick and preserve some marjoram, sage, clover and fennel to feed to your ewes and does after birthing.

19: Garlic planting begins along the Canadian border. In warmer regions, wait until October or November.

20: Dig the tender gladiolus and dahlia bulbs in the North and store them for the winter away from frost and moisture.

21: If you plant your spinach now, it should overwinter and provide an early spring crop.

22: Test the soil of your fall and winter garden as well as of the fields in which you intend to sow winter wheat, rye, alfalfa, canola, clover and timothy.

23: The moon reaches gentle apogee, weakening the power of the full moon (due on the 26th).

24: Now the likelihood of severe heat in the nation's midsection is only half of what it was at the beginning of August. And with the last two cool fronts of August, the chance for frost increases in the northern tier of states.

25: Precipitation is likely before tomorrow's full moon, and this moon will more than likely strengthen the cool front that typically arrives at the end of the month and augment the chances for hurricane formation.

26: The moon is full today. Late August and all of September offer near ideal conditions for dividing and transplanting perennials under the waning moon. Crocus, aconites, snowdrops, daffodils and tulips can go in the ground all across the Northern states; Southern states can wait until October.

27: Greenbrier berries turn blue-black. Rare autumn violets bloom. Except in Northern states, ragweed pollen disappears with the last of the garden phlox. The year's final tier of wildflowers is budding: beggarticks, bur marigolds, asters, zigzag goldenrod.

28: The cool front that crosses the nation in the next few days is the first weather system of Late Summer likely to bring frost across the Northern states.

29: Telephone wires fill with birds as migrations accelerate. Flickers, redheaded woodpeckers, red-winged blackbirds, house wrens, scarlet tanagers, indigo buntings, Eastern bluebirds, robins, grackles and black ducks move south.

30: In the rivers and lakes, lizard's tail drops its leaves. The last firefly blinks in the grass. Puffball mushrooms emerge in moist woodland areas.

31: Burs from the panicled tick trefoil stick to your pants legs and to your pets, sheep and goats.

Almanack Literature
Love Before Cell Phones
By Eleanor Gnandt, Wellington, Ohio

It was during WW II, after being home long enough to get married, my husband of three days had to go to California from Ohio to be shipped out with the Navy.

Two months later, I headed out to be with him, although we knew it would be for a short time. During the war, civilians were put off the buses to make room for service people. What should have been three days became a week, due to my being ousted. Here I was: eighteen years old, never having been away from my parents' home and scared of my own shadow.

Meantime, my husband got a leave and met every bus, but of course I wasn't on any of them. The last afternoon of his leave, I finally arrived. I was supposed to go to the Navy Wives Club who had a room saved for me. However, since I didn't get there when I should have, they gave the room to someone else. They directed me to another organization to see if they could help.

But, thankfully, on my way there, who should I meet but my husband looking for me. The only place we could find to stay was a fleabag-type of hotel, but we were thrilled for it. The next morning, we went back to the Navy Wives, and they had just had an opening for two rooms. We went there and got a nice room.

The icing on the cake was that the other room went to a woman whom I met traveling and we had been together most of the trip. At least I had someone I sort of knew.

My husband returned to his ship that day. He had the phone number and when the shipmates got leave, they would check on me.

Over three weeks went by, and one day my husband showed up. We were together five days when one of his friends called: "So far you've been AWOL but we're shipping out in the morning, and if you're not there, you're a deserter."

Needless to say he went aboard ship, and the following morning they shipped out into the Pacific.

He had a Captain's Court due to the AWOL. The punishment: He was confined to the ship for a month. Apparently the other sailors sided with him because no one left the ship. There really weren't too many places to go!

SEPTEMBER
2018

*Time of crisp and tawny leaves
And of tarnished harvest sheaves,
And of dusty grasses - weeds -
Thistles, with their tufted seeds
Voyaging the Autumn breeze
Like as fairy argosies.*

James Whitcomb Riley

The Gregorian Calendar

S	M	T	W	T	F	S
						1
2	3	4	5	6	7	8
9	10	11	12	13	14	15
16	17	18	19	20	21	22
23	24	25	26	27	28	29
30						

Inventory in Early Autumn

A cardinal sang a little after seven o'clock this morning, sang off and on for about an hour. Crows came and went. Sparrows were chattering outside in the honeysuckles about eight, hummingbirds at work at the feeder.

When I walked the alley after breakfast, I

heard starlings whistling and chattering toward downtown. Sitting in the greenhouse, working in the middle of the morning, I listened to the tapping of a yellow-bellied sapsucker on the siding of the house, an old friend returning from spring on the way back to Tennessee. As I left for the woods, a long, long flock of grackles flew southeast, leading the way.

The sky was so clear, the wind soft. I went beside the water, taking inventory to keep the day: great fields of goldenrod at the height of bloom; the first white small-flowered asters; new chickweed sprouts with two to four leaves spreading across the ground; bare buckeye trees, new buds showing; aging smartweed and snakeroot; blanched wood nettle; seeded wingstem, leaves bleached with powdery mildew.

I saw summer-green ginger leaves; gray brome; dry leaf cup; agrimony seeds crumbling; wood mint dry, still fragrant; field thistles puffed; burdock brittle; last tall coneflowers and last lobelias and last woodland sunflowers and last orange jewelweed; new beggarticks; new burr marigolds bright as April cowslip; low, low river; downy woodpecker chirr and blue jay bell call and kingfisher rattle and nasal peent of the nuthatch and a robin peeping its migration song.

Crows followed me home. There, the climbing virgin's bower still held its blossoms on the redbud tree. The white boneset and the zinnias and New England asters filled the north garden, and cabbage whites and monarchs and painted ladies, buckeyes and red admirals, fritillaries and checkerspots and skippers and swallowtails, honey bees and bumble bees still swarmed around them. Jumpseeds along the front sidewalk still jumped when my fingers stroked them. Craneflies were spinning in the sun. Dragonflies still hunted in the backyard pond. The koi still fed with gusto, their water almost as warm as it had been in July.

The Blackberry Jam Moon and the Jumping Jumpseed Moon

Among the many signs of approaching autumn, the maturing of the jumpseed plant is one of the more dependable. When its flowers have turned to brittle seeds, then the last tier of wildflowers starts to open throughout the country. White and violet asters, orange beggarticks and bur marigolds, late field goldenrod and zigzag goldenrod come into bloom, blending with the last of the purple ironweed, yellow sundrops, blue chicory, golden touch-me-nots, showy coneflowers and great blue lobelias.

September 2: The Blackberry Jam Moon enters its final quarter at 9:37 p.m.

September 7: The moon reaches perigee at 8:21 a.m.

September 9: The Jumping Jumpseed Moon is new at 1:01 p.m.

September 16: The moon enters its second quarter at 6:15 p.m.
September 20: The moon reaches apogee at 7:54 p.m.
September 24: The moon is full at 9:52 p.m.

Meteorology

Weather history suggests that the cold waves of Early Fall usually cross the Mississippi River on or about the following dates: September 2, 8, 12, 15, 20, 24 and 29.

Tornadoes, hail, floods or prolonged periods of soggy pasture are most likely to occur in connection with tropical storms, especially near lunar perigee, September 7, new moon on September 9 and full moon on September 24.

The S.A.D. Stress Index

September's relatively pleasant temperatures and clear skies keep seasonal affective disorder at bay throughout most of the month. In addition, hormonal energy may increase at this time of year, creating an "autumn surge" that combats S.A.D.

Key for Interpreting the S.A.D. Index:
Totals of 100 to 80: Severe stress
79 to 55: Severe to moderate stress
54 to 40: Moderate stress
39 to 25: Light to moderate stress
24 and below: Light stress

Day	Clouds	Weather	Daylight	Moon	Total
September 2:	0	8	9	0	17
September 8:	0	11	10	25	46
September 16:	1	6	11	0	18
September 20:	2	4	12	10	28
September 24:	4	8	13	25	50

The Sun

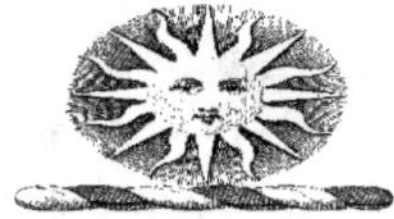

Autumn equinox occurs (and the Sun enters its Middle Autumn sign of Libra) at 8:01 p.m. on September 22. Within several days of that moment, the night is about 12 hours long almost everywhere in the continental United States.

The Planets

♃ ♄ ♂ ♀

Mars in Capricorn and Saturn in Sagittarius move into the southern sky after sundown. Venus in Virgo is the giant evening star in the far west, Jupiter at her heels in Libra in the southwest.

The Stars

With Libra and Scorpio lost in the western horizon, Cygnus, the Northern Cross, with Deneb its brightest star, is a sky guide for autumn, moving slightly west from its central August position. Leading it on, just a little further west, is Lira and its major star, Vega. Below Cygnus lies Aquila and its keystone, Altair.

Peak Activity Times for Creatures

The following guide to lunar position shows when the moon is above (Best times) or below (Second-best times) the country, and, therefore, the period during which livestock, people, fish and game are typically the most active and the hungriest.

Date	Best	Second-Best
September 1:	Midnight to Dawn	Afternoons
September 2 – 8:	Mornings	Evenings
September: 9 – 15:	Afternoons	Midnight to Dawn
September 16 - 23:	Evenings	Mornings
September 24 – 30:	Midnight to Dawn	Afternoons

Calendar of Feast Days and Holidays for Farmers, Gardeners and Homesteaders

September 3, 2018: Labor Day

September 9 – 11, 2018: Rosh Hashanah: Jewish New Year and first High Holiday. Some sub-sects also celebrate the creation of man on this date.

September 11 – October 9, 2018: Al Hijirah/ Muharram: This feast, the Islamic New Year, will continue for 29 days. No religious significance, but like many New Year celebrations, it is a cultural event. A rise in halal sales could be expected during this period.

September 20 – 21, 2018: Ashura: This date commemorates the martyrdom of Muhammad's grandson, Hussein. It also celebrates Noah's survival from the Great Flood.

September 23 – 25, 2018: Harvest Moon Festival: Harvest Moon Festival, Chuseok: Often observed by Korean Americans and others of Asian descent.

The Almanack Daybook
for September of 2018

1: Squirrels shred Osage fruits in the woods. Rose of Sharon, which was bright from Kansas to New York a few weeks ago, has suddenly lost most of its flowers. Japanese knotweed petals darken and fall.

2: The Blackberry Jam Moon enters its weak final quarter this evening. This is also the date of the September 2 weather system, but the moon's weak phase reduces its power.

3: Lunar influence is expected to be low today through the 5th. Take advantage of this period to work with family, pets and livestock, family and clients.

4: As the day moves to within a few degrees of equinox, sycamores, tulip trees, slippery elms, poplars, locust, elms, box elders, buckeyes, dogwoods, chinquapin oaks, lindens and redbuds may begin to show their autumn colors.

5: Autumn apple picking has begun across the North, and the harvest is nearly half over for tobacco, tomato and potato growers in the Southern States. Cottonwoods fade as the goldenrod turns and the soybean fields yellow.

6: Kingbirds, finches, ruddy ducks, herring gulls and yellow-bellied sapsuckers move south. The last young grackles and hummingbirds leave their nests.

7: The moon reaches perigee this morning, beginning a three-day period of strong lunar influence (from perigee, the September 8 cool front and new moon).

8: Today is the average date for a significant high-pressure system to cross the Mississippi River. Yesterday's perigee and tomorrow's new moon are very likely to strengthen this system. Expect precipitation as the front comes through. Near the Canadian border, nighttime temperatures will tumble into the 30s. Hurricanes are likely to come ashore in the Gulf or along the East Coast.

9: The Jumping Jumpseed Moon is new at midday. Frost is more likely tonight and tomorrow night than any other times so far in the second half of the year. Berries are red on the silver olives, orange on the American mountain ash, purple on the pokeweed. Wild cherries have disappeared from their branches. Seed pods of the touch-me-not burst in the wind.

10: The soybean harvest has begun across the northern half of the United States. Cobwebs are everywhere in the woods, and the number of butterflies swells in the gardens. When the days are cool, the cicadas are quiet. On the colder nights, the katydids refuse to chant and the frogs are silent.

11: The waxing moon favors the seeding of winter grains and green manure crops. Test the soil and make corrective lime and fertilizer applications for autumn plantings.

12: Sandhill cranes start to arrive in Midwestern wetlands on their way to the Gulf of Mexico. Doves stop calling before dawn until February.

13: August's boneset goes to seed as the corn silage harvest picks up speed. Aster bloom peaks. In the North, corn is denting, and the whole crop is mature in the South. The cutting of silage has taken over from the second and third cuts of hay; soybeans are turning as well as setting pods.

14: Almost everywhere above the equator, people are digging potatoes, picking commercial and private tomato plants clean. The seasons for everbearing strawberries, plums, pears, watermelons and peaches begin in the North.

15: The cold front that usually brings Early Fall to the Northern states today will be weakened considerably by the moon's position between new and full.

16: The moon enters its gentle second quarter this evening. Between today and September 23, lunar influence will be at its lowest of the month, favoring relatively stable weather (but dry and warm conditions) and low stress.

17: Nearly 200 species of birds have begun to fly south by equinox. Only about 60 migrating species remain above the Ohio Valley, and most of those will be on their way by the close of October.

18: Wood nettle seeds are black and brittle. Throughout the pastures, milkweed pods are ready to open. In the perennial garden, late-blooming hostas discard their petals.

19: Great crested flycatchers, blue-gray gnatcatchers, ruby-throated hummingbirds, eastern wood peewees and bank swallows move south. The cobwebs that blocked summer paths become less common. The wingstem bows to sets its seeds.

20: The moon reaches apogee after sundown, further weakening the power of the moon to influence the high-pressure system that usually crosses the nation near this date. On the other hand, lunar fortunes quickly reverse as the moon reaches the end of its second quarter (on September 24).

21: In the northern half of the United States, the first tier of trees, including the ashes, cottonwoods, box elders, hickories and locusts, turns quickly after equinox.

22: Today is equinox, the sun's halfway position between summer and winter. Poison ivy, sumac and Virginia creeper turn the fencerows red and gold.

23: Precipitation is expected today as the September 24 cool front approaches and the moon becomes full.

24: The moon is full after dark, breaking the stability of middle September and bringing the chance of frost to most of the Northern states and hurricane rains to the Southeast and Lower Midwest.

25: Now as the moon wanes, put in spring bulbs, divide perennials, shrubs and trees.

26: The sugar beet, pear, cabbage and cauliflower harvests commence near this date in the Great Lakes region. In Wisconsin, Massachusetts, New Jersey, Oregon and Washington State, the cranberry harvest begins as berries darken in the cooler weather.

27: Monarch and swallowtail butterflies often become more numerous and visit the last flowers in the afternoon sun.

28: Tree after tree joins in the collapse of year, some foliage turning color overnight. Aster blossoms start to disappear; their departure parallels leaf fall, the end of the insect season, the end of the spiderweb season and an acceleration in bird migration.

29: The final cold front of September, still under the sway of the gibbous moon, is due to reach the Mississippi today, and it increases the possibility of light frost above the Ohio Valley. More signs to accompany the new chill: goldenrod flowers become tufted and gray.

30: Milkweed pods burst. Many black walnut trees are completely bare. Crab apples are thinning. Color spreads across the maples.

Almanack Literature
Nanny and the Lamb
by Bob, Bonnie and Shirley Applegate,
Washington, Iowa

Mother Ewe Number 9 gave birth to two boy lambs at the barn. They were white, and one was bigger than the other. The big one started to push off the little one.

Bob and Bonnie carried the little lamb to the goat shed so he could suck on a nanny goat. In a few days, the lamb would just follow them to the shed.

In a short time, the lamb found an extra-wide space in the fence, and he crawled through the holes to get to the nanny goat. He also found an open space under the loading chute at the barn, and he would go by himself to the goat shed and get breakfast, dinner and supper.

We watched him many times go across the yard by himself, "baaaing" all the way. The nanny would come out of the shed and answer him. He crawled through the fences and would eat, crawl back out and go back to the barn 300 feet away. If it was hot out, he would stop in the shade of a piece of machinery and rest a while.

As time went along, the lamb grew and the hole in the fences got so the lamb could not squeeze through, so he just stayed with the goats and finished growing up, and the nanny did a real good job of raising him!

OCTOBER
2018

In the next century
or the one beyond that,
they say,
are valleys, pastures,
we can meet there in peace
if we make it.
To climb these coming crests
one word to you, to
you and your children:
stay together
learn the flowers
go light

From Gary Snyder's "For the Children"

The Gregorian Calendar

S	M	T	W	T	F	S
	1	2	3	4	5	6
7	8	9	10	11	12	13
14	15	16	17	18	19	20
21	22	23	24	25	26	27
28	29	30	31			

Bearing Witness

In his poem, "For the Children," Gary Snyder advises his readers to "stay together/learn the flowers/go light." The admonition is one of the high points of his 1969 Pulitzer Prize-winning collection of poetry, *Turtle Island*. Written in the early decades of America's slow awakening to the destruction of the Earth by forces of ignorance, apathy and greed, the book is both a celebration of Nature and call to its defense.

Snyder offers less poetic and more radical suggestions in an addendum to *Turtle Island*, his manifesto, "Four Changes," but his advice "For the Children" seems to me the most memorable and practical. It is a sound point of departure as well as an ideal and might be restated in any number of ways: Create and support committed communities. Be aware of what happens in your yard and in the world. Don't waste resources. Try to do no harm.

There are other aspects of ecological responsibility one might consider. "Direct action," say Bill Devall and George Sessions in *Deep Ecology*, "means giving active voice to deep ecological intuitions, encouraging more intuitive insights, as well as acquiring more knowledge and understanding of our bioregion, homeland, Nature and ourselves."

And Greenpeace suggests that a life sensitive to "learning the flowers" creates a fundamental prelude to action: "A person bearing witness must accept responsibility for being aware of an injustice. The person may then choose to do something or stand by, but he may not turn away in ignorance."

The Jumping Jumpseed Moon and the Shattering Ginkgo Moon

Jumpseeds jump and milkweed pods burst, flowers go to seed, and frost season opens across the northern part of the United States. Following a hard freeze, and among the most spectacular doorways between Middle Autumn and Late Autumn is the collapse of the foliage of the ginkgo tree. Often after a cold spell in late October or early November, the ginkgo leaves turn deep gold all at once, and then in a day or so, they shatter suddenly into a gilded coverlet of the ground below.

October 2: The Jumping Jumpseed Moon enters its final quarter at 4:45 a.m.

October 5: The moon reaches perigee at 5:28 p.m.

October 8: The Shattering Ginkgo Moon is new at 10:47 p.m.

October 16: The moon enters its second quarter at 2:01 p.m.

October 17: The moon reaches apogee at 2:16 p.m.

October 24: The moon is full at 11:45 a.m.

October 31: The moon enters its final quarter at 11:40 a.m. It reaches perigee this same date at 3:05 p.m.

Meteorology

Weather history suggests that the cold waves of Middle Fall are likely to cross the Mississippi River on or about October 2, 7, 13, 17, 23 and 30.

Tornadoes, hail, floods or prolonged periods of soggy pasture commonly occur in connection with tropical storms. The period between October 19 and 25 brings an increased chance for dangerous weather, especially in the South.

Lunar perigee on October 5, new moon on October 8 and full moon on October 24 are likely to intensify weather systems near those dates.

The S.A.D. Stress Index

Seasonal affective disorder becomes more frequent in October as the length of the night increases and chances for mild weather decrease. Although cloud cover is ordinarily not a major factor in S.A.D. during middle autumn, the odds for completely overcast conditions rise steadily.

Key for Interpreting the S.A.D. Index:
Totals of 100 to 80: Severe stress
79 to 55: Severe to moderate stress
54 to 40: Moderate stress
39 to 25: Light to moderate stress
24 and below: Light stress

Day	Clouds	Weather	Day	Moon	Totals
October 2:	5	12	14	15	46
October 5:	5	13	14	20	52

October 8:	6	14	15	23	58
October 17:	7	14	17	0	38
October 24:	9	15	19	25	68
October 31:	11	17	20	0	48

The Sun

October 24 is Cross Quarter Day, the halfway mark between autumn equinox and winter solstice. The Sun enters the Late Autumn constellation of Scorpio at the same time.

The Planets

Saturn in Sagittarius, followed by Mars in Capricorn, lies in the south-southwest after the Sun goes down. Venus in Virgo remains the evening star until the middle of the month, when it fades into the sunset Jupiter, in Libra, flirts with the western horizon throughout October, disappearing shortly after Venus.

The Stars

At 11:00 p.m., Cygnus is still high above you in the west, along with late summer's Aquila and Lyra. But the Pleiades and the Hyades of Taurus lie on the eastern horizon, announcing

Middle Autumn. A few hours after midnight, Orion appears in the far east, and it moves to the center of the sky before sunrise.

The Shooting Stars

The Draconid meteors fall at the rate of about ten per hour in the vicinity of the North Star after midnight between October 6 and 10. The dark moon will favor finding these meteors.

The Orionid meteors appear in Orion during the early morning hours of October 21 and 22 at the rate of 15 to 30 per hour. The bright gibbous moon may obscure some of those meteors with its light.

Peak Activity Times for Creatures

The following guide to lunar position shows when the moon is above (Best times) or below (Second-best times) the country, and, therefore, the period during which livestock, people, fish and game are typically the most active and the hungriest.

Date	Best	Second-Best
October 1:	Midnight to Dawn	Afternoons
October 2 – 7:	Mornings	Evenings
October: 8 – 15:	Afternoons	Midnight to Dawn
October 16 - 23:	Evenings	Mornings
October 24 – 31:	Midnight to Dawn	Afternoons

Calendar of Feast Days and Holidays for Farmers, Gardeners and Homesteaders

October 9 – 18, 2018: **Navaratri /Navadurgara:** This Hindu feast honors the goddess Durga. Female animals are typically not used for this celebration.

The Almanack Daybook for October of 2018

1: Seed winter greens and winter grains while the moon is dark (the next ten days).

2: The Jumping Jumpseed Moon enters its weak final quarter, moderating the first cold front of October.

3: Even before all the leaves come down, "second spring" is underway, regreening pastures, bottomlands and fencerows. Wood mint grows new stalks. Watercress revives. Waterleaf reappears. April's sweet Cicely, May's sweet rockets, ragwort, dock and poison hemlock, June's cinquefoil and hollyhocks, July's avens and caraway, September's zigzag goldenrod and small-flowered asters send up fresh leaves. The grass continues to grow, glowing in the low sun. Newly planted winter wheat creates patches of emerald green in the countryside.

4: The waning moon is favorable for pruning shrubs or trees to retard growth and for killing weeds. Also complete autumn culling of sheep and goats before pasture season comes to a close.

5: The moon reaches perigee today, increasing the possibility that the October 7 cold front will bring frost across the Northern states.

6: In the swamps, skunk cabbage comes up again. In the garden, red knuckles of rhubarb sometimes push to the surface. Ginkgo fruits, which will be on the ground by late November, turn pink.

7: Peak leafturn starts to occur in woodlots where maples, ashes, buckeyes, wild cherry and locusts predominate. Many Osage leaves are yellow now, a few ginkgoes starting to fade. Cottonwoods and the rest of the box elders lose their leaves, and great openings form in the high canopy.

8: The Shattering Ginkgo Moon is new today, setting a chilly platform for the arrival of Middle Fall in just a few days. Under the dark moon, plants and bulbs intended for spring forcing should be placed in light soil now and stored in a place where temperatures remain cool (but not freezing).

9: Expect relatively mild temperatures and precipitation as the barometer falls in advance of the October 13 cold front. Terns and meadowlarks, yellow-rumped warblers and purple martins migrate south. Chimney swifts, wood thrushes, barn swallows and red-eyed vireos join them as Early Fall moves to a close.

10: Fencerows are shedding the leaves of poison ivy and Virginia creeper. Grape vines hold on yellow green.

11: Half of the winter wheat is normally in the ground by now just as beech leaves rust at the edges.

12: The tips of many spruce trees are putting on fresh growth, forecasting spring.

13: Middle Fall begins near this date. The coldest morning so far in the season often occurs as the October 13 cold front arrives. This front is the first front to bring a chance of snow flurries at average elevations along the 40th Parallel.

14: Migrating robins feed on the honeysuckle berries. Water willow yellows by the rivers.

15: The heaviest time of Halloween market sales begins in the middle of October as rutting time begins for deer along the 40th Parallel.

16: The moon enters its gentle second quarter today, and temperatures, which dipped at the arrival of Middle Fall, should now start to rise.

17: The moon reaches apogee, contributing to the warm-up, and stable weather conditions are likely for several days throughout the nation.

18: In the cooler, wetter nights, crickets and katydids are weakening, but woolly bear caterpillars appear on back roads when the sun warms the pavement. Monarch butterflies have left the Midwest. Only a few swallowtails and fritillaries visit the garden, and just a few fireflies glow in the grass.

19: In Northern states, mulch root crops to keep them from turning to mush when the ground freezes solid.

20: Peak leaf color usually starts to fade today in the East and Middle Atlantic states. Peak leaf coloring is just beginning, however, in the middle and southern Appalachians.

21: Soil temperatures have ordinarily fallen into the 50s, and pasture growth slows. The chance for light snow increases as full moon and the October 23 high-pressure system approaches.

22: Process honey from your hives, leaving plenty for the bees. Schedule garlic planting.

23: Some ginkgoes are green, others fully gold and losing foliage; they will drop their leaves overnight as the Shattering Ginkgo Moon departs early in November.

24: One year in three brings frost with the October 23 cold front above the Border States, and today's full moon is very likely to strengthen that front.

25: Silver maples are champagne gold, and the sugar and red maples are down or are shedding quickly. Tulip trees are almost bare. Morning fogs become more common.

26: Harvest continues all around the country, with about half of the corn and three-fourths of the soybeans cut.

27: In the cranberry regions of the country, most of the berries have been brought in from the bogs.

28: Fertilize the lawn as the moon wanes. Then feed the trees after all their leaves are down.

29: High pollen counts are over in most of the country until Early Spring.

30: The last weather system of the month, strengthened by tomorrow's lunar perigee, comes across the country with Halloween.

31: The last cabbage butterflies look for cabbages. At night, crickets take the place of katydids.

Almanack Literature
Duck Killer
By Susan Perkins from Hardtimes Farm, Kentucky

Two summers ago, my daughter-in-law Brandi came running into the house screaming, "I think a snake's getting the baby ducks!"

My daughter Laurie and I jumped up and ran

out to the shed where Brandi said she heard a bunch of glass breaking. A mother duck had made her nest in a cardboard box stored on the top of some wooden shelves used for storing my canning jars.

It was real dark in the shed, but I could make out part of a snake in the filtered light that made its way through the oak boards covering the building. When our eyes became adjusted to the dark, we could not believe what we saw.

A huge, and I mean huge, cow snake had coiled around the mother duck twice and was squeezing the life out of her. His intention was not to eat her, but rather all her newly hatched babies. The mother duck must have fought him like the devil to cause him to try to kill her. And kill he would have, if I hadn't grabbed his tail, startling him enough to uncoil, allowing the duck to break free. The snake disappeared through the cracks in the floor, falling beneath the building.

Three of the babies were dead, crushed from the fight that had taken place. If I hadn't seen it with my own eyes, I would never have believed a snake could kill a big duck by playing python. We moved mother and the remaining babies to a safe location, as I was sure the snake would return to finish the job.

NOVEMBER
2018

Look to the Great Harvest
When all Things will bear Fruit and
Will be ready for the Gathering.

Paracelsus

The Gregorian Calendar

S	M	T	W	T	F	S
				1	2	3
4	5	6	7	8	9	10
11	12	13	14	15	16	17
18	19	20	21	22	23	24
25	26	27	28	29	30	

Hiding Under the
Starling Murmuration Moon

As the last leaves of the year come down, seed catalogs arrive in my mailbox, and I plan for May under the new November moon. Usually, I order a few packages of geraniums, coleus and petunias, and I start them under grow lights close to the furnace, which happens to be in the attic.

If I keep the soil warm, moist and close enough to the fluorescent bulbs, the seeds germinate within a week or so and then develop steadily throughout the winter.

Although I enjoy the flowers that the plants produce in spring and summer, for me, the best part of sprouting seeds in winter is sitting next to them, feeling safe and disconnected from the snow and from the rest of my life.

There, the only sound is the low purr of the furnace fan. All around me and the plants and the soft lights, the space is dark and private. The smell of new earth thins the musty smell of the attic. I hide, shielded by a comforter that feels part childhood, part angel.

My eyes and, it seems, my longing search the magical glowing green of the sprouts for meaning. All their prophetic power rests in their two or four leaves, all of their potential compressed into the most delicate and vulnerable flesh.

Here there is no thought of maturity or harvest, no logical conclusion, no socially redeeming value, no death. I do not think about the eventual work of transplanting and mulching, conflicts with insects and weather and blights. Even the promise of beauty, color and fragrance is irrelevant. Only the coverlet of this time in this place with these creatures makes sense.

The Shattering Ginkgo Moon and the Starling Murmuration Moon

Starlings are among the earliest birds to gather in flocks after their fledglings have left the nest. Even in Middle Summer, small groups dive and soar through the air, all the birds seeming to perform their acrobatics as a single creature. Larger and larger flocks form as winter settles in, and great "murmurations" (the name for a flock of starlings that flies and plays in unison) can be seen zooming up then down and around above cut-over fields.

November 7: The Shattering Ginkgo Moon becomes the new Starling Murmuration Moon at 11:02 a.m.

November 14: The moon reaches apogee at 10:57 a.m.

November 15: The moon enters its second quarter at 10:03 a.m.

November 23: The moon is full at 12:39 a.m.

November 26: The moon reaches perigee at 7:10 a.m.

November 29: The moon enters its final quarter at 7:19 p.m.

Meteorology

Weather history suggests that the cold waves of Late Fall usually cross the Mississippi River on or about November 2, 6, 11, 16, 20, 24 and 28. Snow or rain often occurs prior to the passage of each major front.

If strong storms occur this month, weather patterns suggest that they will happen during the following periods: November 2 – 5, 14 – 16 and November 22 – 27 .

It is probable that the new moon on November 7, full moon on November 23 and lunar perigee on November 26 will bring stronger-than-average storms to the United States, complicating Thanksgiving travel.

The S.A.D. Stress Index

The average length of November's night is almost as great as the night's length in December and January; the weather becomes more severe, and clouds thicken. S.A.D. increases to winter levels and the effect of lunar phase and position becomes even more significant.

Key for Interpreting the S.A.D. Index:

Totals of 100 to 80: Severe stress
79 to 55: Severe to moderate stress
54 to 40: Moderate stress
39 to 25: Light to moderate stress
24 and below: Light stress

Day	Clouds	Weather	Day	Moon	Totals
November 1:	13	17	22	0	52
November 7:	14	18	23	20	75
November 14:	16	19	23	0	58
November 23:	17	20	24	25	86
November 26:	18	21	24	20	83
November 29:	20	21	25	10	76

The Sun

On November 23, the Sun enters the Early Winter sign of Sagittarius. At the end of November, sunset has reached to within just a few minutes of its earliest time throughout the nation. The latest sunrise, however, is still about half an hour away.

Daylight Saving Time ends at 2:00 a.m. on Sunday, November 4. Set clocks back one hour at 2:00 a.m.

The Planets

♃ ♄ ♂ ♀

Now in Aquarius, Mars is visible in the southwestern sky after sundown. Venus reappears early this month in the east as the morning star. Jupiter is not visible this month, but he joins Venus in Libra in December. Saturn in Sagittarius skims the western horizon at dusk.

The Stars

Late Autumn brings back Orion as an easy marker of sky time. By 11:00 p.m., it has emerged from the east, following a cluster of seven stars, the Pleiades and the red eye of Taurus, Aldebaran. A few hours before dawn, all those stars have moved to fill up the southern sky.

The Shooting Stars

The Taurid shower brings only a handful of meteors per hour on November 4 and 5, and the crescent moon should not interfere with meteor watching. The Leonids (at the rate of about 15 per hour) should be more rewarding. Watch for them near the constellation Leo after midnight on November 17 and 18.

Peak Activity Times for Creatures

The following guide to lunar position shows when the moon is above (Best times) or below (Second-best times) the country, and, therefore, the period during which livestock, people, fish and game are typically the most active and the hungriest.

Date	Best	Second-Best
November 1 - 6:	Mornings	Evenings
November: 7– 15:	Afternoons	Midnight to Dawn
November 16 – 22:	Evenings	Mornings
November 23 – 29;	Midnight to Dawn	Afternoons
November 30:	Mornings	Evenings

Calendar of Feast Days and Holidays for Farmers, Gardeners and Homesteaders

November 21, 2018: Muhammad's Birthday (Mawlid Al-Nabi): Sunni Muslims celebrate Muhammad's birthday today.

November 22, 2018: Thanksgiving

November 26, 2018: Muhammad's Birthday (Mawlid Al-Nabi): Shia Muslims celebrate Muhammad's birthday on this date.

The Almanack Daybook
for November of 2018

1: Late bulbs, garlic, shrubs and trees can be planted in November throughout much of the nation. In Northern states, it might be more practical, however, to plant as soon as possible, preferably before the weather turns much chillier around November 4.

2: Record highs for November are almost always set during the first days of the month; the chances for an afternoon in the 60s or 70s actually increase by 30 percent over those of the last week of October. As the moon wanes throughout this week, prepare to seed your earliest bedding plants for 2018 in a warm location under lights.

3: Cabbage worms still eat the cabbage. Some years, houseflies still find their way indoors. Crickets sing in the milder afternoons and nights. A few butterflies hunt for flowers. Grasshoppers are still common.

4: Major bird migrations through the Midwest and East end in November's first week. Wind speed increases to its winter level. Clouds lie lower in the sky, and the percentage of sunny days drops twenty percent from October's peak.

Across the North, most tree lines show almost no color. Only an occasional Osage gives life to the horizon. In town, however, willows are only half turned. Decorative pears are a deep red, prolonging Middle Fall all in the cities. Dogwoods are pink, magnolias gold for a few days longer. Gum and beech are still full color. Beneath them, privet and spicebush will remain strong throughout much of the month. Silver maples seem to be untouched by the radical shift in the season; they hold until the nights go into the teens.

Gardeners should test the soil and mow the lawn for the last time. Farmers should plant the final winter wheat and complete the harvest of corn, sugar beets and soybeans.

5: Late Fall, a three-to-four-week transition period of chilly temperatures and killing frosts, usually arrives by today along the 40th Parallel. Now is also the pivotal time for autumn cloud cover to intensify darker skies continue through February.

6: The cold front that usually arrives around November 5 – 7 will likely be strengthened by tomorrow's new moon. Precipitation will precede that front. The end of Daylight Saving Time on November 4 will contribute to a rise in seasonal stress as the early dark evenings increase the effects of the moon and the weather.

7: The Shattering Ginkgo Moon, having brought down almost all the golden ginkgoes in the nation, becomes the Starling Murmuration Moon today and will end what is normally the mildest time of the month.

8: From today through the 20th is the normal rutting period for whitetail deer in the central part of the country. Rutting is thought to contribute to an increase in the number of accidents involving cars and deer. Half of those incidents happen between 6:00 p.m. and midnight, and almost all of them occur when weather conditions are mild and clear. The early evenings of Standard Time will increase the likelihood of accidents involving deer.

9: Throughout the nation, practically all weeds and wildflowers become dormant.

10: Mock orange and forsythia are thinning; their leaf-fall measures the progress of the last phase of autumn.

11: Honeysuckles weaken, berries becoming more prominent. Across the countryside, most of the woodlots are dark and empty.

12: Plan frost seeding in January. Fertilize pastures for improved winter hardiness and stimulation of growth in Early Spring. Feed trees and shrubs. Remove tops from everbearing raspberries. Supplies should be on hand for the bedding plant season, which usually begins with the first pansies and begonias under the new November and December moons.

13: Sugar maples, burned by frost, gradually drop their foliage. Almost every junco has arrived for winter. Indoors, older Christmas cacti are budding or even blooming. In the fields, most winter wheat has sprouted. In the garden, mulch strawberries with straw.

14: The moon reaches apogee this morning. Apogee, combined with the moon's weak position between full and new should diminish the power of the cold front which usually crosses the United States in the middle of the month.

15: The moon enters its second quarter this morning. Feed the lawn so that the winter's rain and snow, freezing and thawing, will gently work the fertilizer through the soil. Mulch perennial beds after watering to prevent drying and cold damage.

16: The poinsettia crop is typically shipped by this week. Christmas cacti in bloom are on display in stores.

17: Colors deepen in the swamp. Protected by the flowing water, cress brightens; dock and ragwort grow back beside the dead field grasses.

18: Beech, honeysuckles, boxwood, Osage, pears, sycamores and the strongest of the maples keep scattered color in the landscape past Thanksgiving. Transplant some of your herbs in pots; bring them inside for winter seasonings. Wrap young transplants to protect them against frost cracking. Clean up the last of the garden.

19: The fifth significant cold wave of November is due to cross your land within the next three days, and this is a front that carries snow to the North four years in a decade. Throughout the nation, precipitation is likely before Thanksgiving.

20: Many Northern pastures have stopped growing, and some owners are feeding hay to livestock at this point in the year.

21: The first rutting period for deer usually ends around this time of the month.

22: Today is normally a pivot day for the arrival of much colder weather. The Sun has now moved to within two degrees of solstice, and it enters the Early Winter sign of Sagittarius today.

23: The moon is full early this morning, making it likely that Thanksgiving will be a chilly one.

24: Above the Border States, chances for an afternoon in the 70s are now only one in 100. On March 2, they rise again.

25: This is the date of the latest recorded killing frost in the Lower Midwest.

26: The moon reaches perigee near sunrise. Perigee so close to full moon is likely to complicate the last day of Thanksgiving travel with cold and snow.

27: In warmer climates like southern California, daisy trees and golden sennas are in bloom. Pink blossoms appear on the silk floss trees and maroon and ivory flowers on the Dutchman's pipe vine. In the Southwest, the cascalote trees are blooming. In Baton Rouge, the exotic gingers are still open.

28: In the more northerly woods, second spring, the late greening of the undergrowth, is halted by November's most bitter weather. The most stubborn leaves fall, and the pods of thimble plants explode in the winds.

29: The moon enters its final quarter this morning. As it reaches a weak position between full and new, the moon is likely to contribute to a softening of the harsh Thanksgiving weather and allow a slight warm-up for the first days of December.

30: The last bulb planting (including the garlic crop) and perennial transplanting should be done in anticipation of the arrival of Early Winter.

Almanack Literature
My Hero, My First Love
By Eunice Hicks, Willard, Ohio

When my friend Sallie and I were working on a muck farm, we asked the boss if we could use the outhouse. He said that we could, and he added, "Go down the path, up the road, and across the ditch. You can't miss it."

We thanked him and started down the path. Then we looked and saw an outhouse much closer than the one our boss had told us about.

But we found out when we got to the road that we would also have to go across a ditch to get to the outhouse.

My friend said to me, "You go first. I'll follow you."

I took one step and I slid into the ditch up to my hips in the muck and water.

I screamed and hollered, "Help me! I'm freezing!"

Sallie stopped a man in a car. He saw I needed help, waded into the muck and water, took me by my arms and pulled me from the ditch.

I was so cold and freezing, shaking like a leaf! This man took me and my friend home. As he started to leave, I asked him, "Would you mind telling me your name?"

"Just call me George," he said. Then he laughed.

Sallie and I waved and said thanks. As he drove away, I said to Sallie, "I know that man. I recognized him by his voice. He was my first date in high school!"

Sally and I laughed and laughed until we couldn't laugh any more

DECEMBER
2018

Now I have told the year from dawn to dusk,
Its morning and its evening and its noon;
Once round the sun our slanting orbit rolled,
Four times the season changed, thirteen the moon....

Vita Sackville-West

The Gregorian Calendar

S	M	T	W	T	F	S
						1
2	3	4	5	6	7	8
9	10	11	12	13	14	15
16	17	18	19	20	21	22
23	24	25	26	27	28	29
30	31					

A Wreath for Spring

Having been raised to begin a liturgical year with the first Sunday of Christian Advent, a four-week vigil for Christmas, I usually try to shape some part of my winter around a traditional Advent Wreath.

By the end of November, most of the beech leaves and the Osage leaves have come down, and only a few Bradford pears hold color. The crows are the only birds to call before sunrise, and the local geese have taken up their solemn afternoon processions from field to water. I could settle into winter now, but I prefer to look to spring.

Twelve weeks from now, Late Winter cedes to Early Spring throughout the East and Lower Midwest. Pussy willows catkins are cracking by then, and white tips of snowdrops have emerged from the mulch and skunk cabbage has opened. Purple cress has budded along the river, Cardinals sing before sunrise. Sandhill cranes fly north. Flocks of robins arrive to begin their mating chorus.

And if I place a cluster of twelve candles (instead of four) on the dining room table, lighting one each week from the end of November forward, I keep a semblance of my childhood ritual while creating another procession toward the end of the cold. By the time the last candle is burning, the sky is no longer dark when I have supper at six o'clock.

Bedding plant seeding starts a few days before the new moon (December 7), and I will add to the candle ritual by starting a few seeds then. My sprouting place is near the furnace in the attic. I set up two grow lights and hang them low, leaving space for flats above them maybe three or four inches. I am partial to geraniums and banana seeds this early in the season. Outriders of aconites and crocus, the new sprouts pace the lengthening day, replacing candles in February, opening the door to March and April.

The Flowering Jessamine Moon

Even as most leafdrop and blooming ends across the Northern states, the flowering of bright yellow Jessamine marks the opening of spring in fencerows and lowlands throughout the states that border the Gulf of Mexico. Although the Jessamine flowers are not a fixture of Northern areas, their appearance opens the long encroachment of new life against the frozen barrier of winter.

December 7: The Flowering Jessamine Moon is new at 2:20 a.m.

December 12: The moon reaches apogee at 7:25 a.m.

December 15: The moon enters its second quarter at 6:49 a.m.

December 22: The moon is full at 12:48 p.m.

December 24: The moon reaches perigee at 4:52 a.m.

December 29: The moon enters its final quarter at 4:34 a.m.

Meteorology

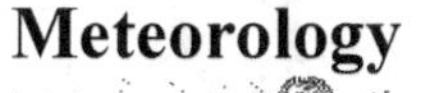

Weather history suggests that the cold waves of Early Winter usually cross the Mississippi River on or about December 2, 8, 15, 20, 25 and 29. Snow or rain often occur prior to the passage of each major front.

If strong storms occur this month, weather patterns suggest that they will happen during the following periods: December 1 – 3, 24 – 26, 31 – January 1. It is probable that new moon on December 7, full moon on December 22 and lunar perigee on December 24 will bring stronger-than-average storms to the United States.

The S.A.D. Stress Index

The shortest days of the year, the increase in cloud cover, and the growing cold all combine with the influence of the moon to produce high S.A.D. Index readings throughout the month.

Key for Interpreting the S.A.D. Index:
Totals of 100 to 80: Severe stress
79 to 55: Severe to moderate stress
54 to 40: Moderate stress
39 to 25: Light to moderate stress
24 and below: Light stress

Day	Clouds	Weather	Day	Moon	Totals
December 1:	21	20	24	0	65
December 7:	23	23	25	20	91
December 12:	23	23	25	10	81
December 15:	24	23	25	0	72
December 22:	24	24	25	25	98
December 29:	25	25	25	5	80

The Sun

Winter solstice occurs at 5:23 p.m. on December 21. The Sun enters the Deep Winter constellation of Capricorn on the same day.

On December 24, the Sun begins to move toward summer solstice, but the days do not actually start to lengthen until December 26.

The Planets

Mars, in Aquarius, lies against the western horizon after dark. Venus in Libra, followed by Jupiter in Ophiuchus, rise from the east before dawn. Saturn in Sagittarius disappears from the night sky by the middle of the month.

The Stars

Orion looms in the east a few hours after dark and remains dominant throughout the nights of early and middle winter. The farther west it moves by 11:00 p.m., the closer spring becomes.

The Shooting Stars

The Geminid meteor show peaks on December 13 – 14 near Gemini, with the crescent moon interfering only a little with meteor viewing. The Ursid Meteors fall after midnight at the rate of about five to ten per hour on December 21 and 22, but bright full moonlight is likely to obscure many of them.

Peak Activity Times for Creatures

The following guide to lunar position shows when the moon is above (Best times) or below (Second-best times) the country, and, therefore, the period during which livestock, people, fish and game are typically the most active and the hungriest.

Date	Best	Second-Best
December 1 – 6:	Mornings	Evenings
December: 7– 14:	Afternoons	Midnight to Dawn
December 15 – 21:	Evenings	Mornings
December 22 – 29;	Midnight to Dawn	Afternoons
December 30 – 31:	Mornings	Evenings

Calendar of Feast Days and Holidays for Gardeners, Farmers and Homesteaders

December 2 – 10: Hanukkah: Festival of Light: This festival is eight days long and offers many possibilities to market.

December 25: Christmas: Milk-fed lambs and kids below 20 pounds are favored for this market.

The Almanack Daybook
for December of 2018

1: Precipitation is expected to precede the first December cold front, due in the first days of the month.

2: Sunset now occurs at the earliest time of the year in the Lower Midwest; it will remain at that time until the middle of December. In the woods, whitetail deer enter their secondary rutting period, which lasts approximately two weeks.

3: Summer's pokeweed stalks burst in the night cold. Milkweed seeds scatter along the roadsides. At the arrival of the early December cold front, eaves often fall overnight from the silver maple, pear and beech trees.

4: Craneflies spin in the afternoon sun. Where snow has melted, moss is still bright green on rotting logs. A few red raspberry leaves and a few red honeysuckle berries hold on. A few sweet gum seed balls continue to swing in the wind. Along the Gulf Coast, Canada geese arrive from the North.

5: Osage fruits lie yellowing, scattered across the ground. Black walnut hulls, shredded by squirrels, stain porches and driveways.

6: Early Winter, the first period of consistently cold temperatures before solstice, often begins about this time. Tomorrow's new moon increases the chances that the entry of that season will be strong.

7: The Flowering Jessamine Moon is new early this morning. As this moon grows throughout December, it pulls spring up from the Gulf of Mexico, bringing jasmine into flower throughout the South, even as it pushes the coldest weather of the year to Northern regions.

8: Most second flowering of forsythia is finished. Basal leaf clusters of carnations, sweet rockets, celandine, garlic mustard, poppies, lamb's ear and daisies remain green underneath the snow.

9: Ducks complete migration from Northern waters. Brown Pelicans nest in Louisiana.

10: Order pasture seeds and schedule pasture frost seeding for January and February, the time that the dramatic thaws of Early Spring can occur well into the North.

11: In southern Florida, mango trees are in full bloom and will produce fruit for harvest in late June through August. Ruby red grapefruits are ready to eat in the groves north of Miami.

12: Lunar apogee occurs this morning, weakening the power of the new moon to influence weather. The period between today and December 15, when the moon enters its second quarter, should dilute the cold of the past week.

13: Along the 40th Parallel, the sun begins to set later, starting its movement toward summer. But double-digit below-zero lows now become possible as far south as the Ohio Valley.

14: Brown-barked river birches and white birches contrast with the black trunks of oaks and elms. Red-twigged dogwoods stand out against the snow.

15: The moon enters its second quarter this morning, softening the effects of the December 15 cold front. Deer mating time gradually comes to a close, decreasing the likelihood that erratic deer behavior will cause automobile accidents.

16: The gull migration, the last major bird migration activity, ends near this date. In the Southeast, mistletoe becomes visible as the high trees lose all their leaves.

17: Fallen leaves are matting down from the rain and snow, their bright middle-autumn colors gone, faded to a uniform, dull brown.

18: In warm years, crocus may be pushing up through their mulch. A few pussy willow catkins could be opening.

19: Odds against the survival of Northern garden vegetables rise sharply as the December 20 cold approaches.

19 – 25: These are the shortest days of the year throughout the nation.

20: The December 20 cold front is one of the two "white Christmas" fronts. Since it will arrive near full moon, chances for snow increase.

21: Today is winter solstice. Begin to track the Sun's movement towards June by measuring how far sunlight enters a south window today. You will see it retreat relatively quickly in the month ahead.

22: The moon is full in the early afternoon, adding lunar force to the cold fronts that almost always cross the United States on or about December 20 and 25.

23: Starting today, the day begins and ends a little bit farther to the north every 24 hours. This movement does not translate into a shorter night until December 26.

24: The moon reaches perigee early this morning, strengthening the Christmas cold front and increasing the chances for a white Christmas throughout the North.

25: Meteorological conditions remain challenging for the next few days until the moon gradually moves farther from Earth and approaches its final quarter.

26: The days begin to lengthen.

27: The tufted titmice begin mating calls.

28: Prepare flats, containers and grow lights for the seeding of bedding plants at new moon on January 5 of 2019.

29: The moon enters its final quarter today, softening the final cold front of 2018.

30: Since the moon will not turn new until January 5, it will be relatively weak throughout the long New Year's weekend.

31: Lunar influence on the weather should be light until early the middle of the week ahead, favoring the close of holiday travel. New Year's Eve will be wet, but the first cold front of 2019 is likely to be relatively mild.

Almanack Literature
It Takes a Village to Raise a Calf
By E. Bridgewater, Scottsburg, Indiana

We live on a farm and raise beef cows. We rotate them on pasture here at the farm and then across the road where we have more pasture. In the crossover, if we miss a calf that is not with its mother, the mother will go back to the gate and bawl until her baby is found.

One time, I stayed in the truck and my husband went over the hill to find the cows and their calves. After a long time, I saw the two calves coming up, then a little while later, the cows were coming up the hill.

But no husband.

Just when I was ready to go looking for him, here he came with a baby calf.

This is his story: He found the cows and calves, and they all started up the hill back toward the road. All of a sudden the cows break and run to the right and back down the hill. My husband got mad, really mad! He picked up a big stick!

The cows stood with their heads down to the ground, and then they looked at him, then they looked back at the ground. When he got over to them, he saw what they are looking at: a tiny baby calf.

The baby's mother, not being very motherly, had crossed over to the farm and didn't look back, but when her baby was carried over to the barn and it let out a loud cry, she came running and was a good mother forever after.

Valediction for the Year

Grounding in just what lies around me,
learning to understand home,
feeling the limits of independence,
the solitude of landscape,
finding enough
in plain observations and events,
embracing the ordinary, expecting nothing more,
accepting this particular passage
of time and location in time,
seeing salvation in the commonplace,
marking the sunlight of solstice on my wall,
counting pussy willows,
measuring the height of winter snowdrops,
asking nothing more than these pure acts,
allowing, opening, watching the finite visions
that contain no transcendence,
no special compensation,
considering the precision of each fragment
that names the exact place of Earth's orbit
and my exact place within it now.

Bill Felker

Bill Felker has been writing *Poor Will's Almanack* for papers and magazines since 1984, and he has published annual almanacks since 2003. His radio version of *Poor Will* is broadcast weekly on NPR station WYSO and is available on podcast at **www.wyso.org**.

For more information, visit Bill Felker's phenology website at **www.poorwillsalmanack.com**.

www.ingramcontent.com/pod-product-compliance
Lightning Source LLC
Chambersburg PA
CBHW071215240726
48654CB00009B/791